The UFO Armageddon

The
UFO
Armageddon

The Real Untruths about Space Visitors

An extraterrestrial entertainment

by

Brian Thomas

About the Author

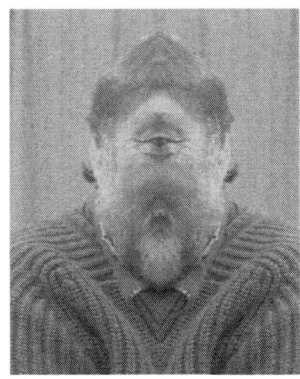

WHEN he first landed on Earth, the author of this fine little tome, whose 1,456-letter Ataclantasta Cluster name is too complex to either print or pronounce but sounds like *"Mip,"* decided to adopt a low profile by becoming a freelance juggling unicyclist.

Lacking the required balance, he instead became the caretaker of a wool sorting pergola in isolated rural Cranberry, a windswept wasteland not unlike his former home, a star system which lies (and sometimes truths) many light years away in the Twiddlysome Constellation. This exotic constellation was named after Blinkstow University emeritus of Tittletattle, Prof Euripides Twiddlysome of Crone, founder of the Bladge School of Interstellar Cartography and Cutlery Bending, who discovered the galactic zone whilst peering skyward through an empty pepper pot on a crisp October morning in 1973 during a coach trip to Anglesey.

Of the author's previous books, the first, *On Entering the Atmosphere*, describing his arrival on planet Earth in a cloud of steam and meteor grit, sold four copies and was remaindered within 22 minutes. His second title, *From the Cluster to Here*, was pulped on the first morning but contained some piercing observations of Earth life, including the reflection that it was "a bit of a doddle."

In his latest work he has concentrated on a rare publication, lost to the sands of time and indifference, which rings a deep, personal chord for him as a fellow astral traveller. This diminutive account contains a revisiting of some of the rare *UFO Armageddon* magazine's seminal articles, culled from a back catalogue of 32 waste bins, two skips and a woollen sock.

Enjoy!

About the Cover

Our cover illustration (*from TUFOA issue #27b*) – which is here displayed in full – shows how Space and Time can collide with seemingly reckless abandon.

In this Meredith Bharp sketch of the ancient carved sarcophagus lid from Palenque, Mexico, the stonework "clearly shows" the renowned 7th Century ruler Lord Pakal The Great (*K'inich Janaab' Pakal*) astride a 20th Century Honda 50 (*Hh'onnda Fiftii*).

The artist further suggests that the skillfully-sculpted yet anachronistic motorised scooter is the result of a "mysterious time displacement trigger, moulded by the rarely-observed Harpse-Bandsaw Epoch Dilation Gas-Pond Wobble Effect."

But what do you think readers?

Write what you think in this (inner) space, study, evaluate, and then discard.
[Also useful for storing small shopping lists and elusive telephone numbers.]

Preface: Roadmap!

On March 7, 1962, three men entered the Lima grocery store of Miguel Dozo in coastal Peru. They looked ordinary enough at first: neat blue suits, striped ties, white shirts, black patent leather shoes. It was only when one of them spoke that Miguel noticed that the stranger's mouth was in his forehead. In shrill, unearthly voices the trio demanded three sacks of chickpeas and a road map of Birmingham.

When Miguel told them he stocked neither chickpeas nor road maps, the men became agitated and, as they left empty-handed, each pinched the shopkeeper's nose gently and told him to watch the constellation of Orion. Miguel did so for three months until he developed a serious left-eye twitch and was forced to wear a monocle.

Shortly after this, Miguel was visited by an assortment of winged creatures, dwarfs in silver suits, bilingual fish and a choir of green-skinned reptiles with tails who claimed to be milkmen. On July 15 Miguel had his final visitors: two men in white coats who took him away to a farm where people laugh a lot.

But was Miguel Dozo mad?

Or was he just another victim of the coming **UFO Armageddon**?

Dozo captures an image of one of his multitude of abductors

Could this be the pie man that Simple Simon met – an image lightly scratched on an ancient ice cream cart at historic Sacsayhuaman in Peru? Could he be from another galaxy?

The Journal!

The popular but now-defunct extraterrestrial magazine *The UFO Armageddon* was created by identical twins Maurice and Adelbald Slump on a work bench at the rear of their garage in the mid-1980s.

The Slumps (*pictured below*) warned that the sheer number, intensity and "scary-freakiness" of global UFO sightings recorded by Ufologists, scientists, pilots and "them ord'nary folk" would lead to planetary Armageddon, the end of Mankind, and "a lot of nasty fireworks and stuff." They named their magazine accordingly. Then, more sensibly, they named it *The UFO Armageddon*. Both were convinced that the plague of "sightings" from around the world presaged a final inter-species conflict (or at least, a bit of a cosmic dust-up).

Their periodical soon took off (vertically) and became the 97th most popular UFO journal in South Wiltshire, following closely on the narrative heels of the glossy ten-page *Blobs in the Sky Quarterly* (SawSir Bulletins) and the fortnightly mimeographed *That's Not A Cloud!* (Over-the-Chippie Free Press).

An early newspaper cutting from *Phlegm's Weekly* that reported the Slumps' fledgling literary project suggested the twins had each taken biochemistry courses at the University of Smee. But later investigations revealed that, though well versed in alien mythology, the Slumps had been less than truthful about their background and were in fact sewer, ditch and gully cleaners (appropriately jobtitled **U**ndersurface **F**resheriser **O**peratives) employed by Herbifordshire Council.

This "outing" never deterred them, and their colourful, enthusiastic and increasingly outrageous periodical appeared on newsstands for more than a decade – until around 2000* when the brothers ceased publication after a particularly divisive custard fight. Their chief researcher, Chappie "Off Road" Bonscatho (a short biography of whom appears later), had already left them two years earlier to concentrate on overhauling trombones.

*Dates often conflict in the UFOA record and several magazines often bore the wrong month and issue number. No attempt has been made to correct these errors.

"My bad dream" by artist Adelbald Slump, drawn after the twins' break-up and a week of eating nothing but pomegranates

UFOA: Carol, can you tell us your UFO experience?
Carol: I saw *three* ships. Sailing by!
UFOA: And when was this?
Carol: On Christmas Day!
UFOA: About what time?
Carol: On Christmas Day in the morning.
Carol Christmas recounts her extraterrestrial encounter.

OUR
SKIES
ARE
PACKED
WITH
FEAR
AND
MENACE

the UFO Armageddon

ISSUE #19 JUNE 97
Just £1   Quote: A51

PRIME MINISTER MEETS ALIENS: OFFERS SAFE HAVEN IN WILTSHIRE!

Village Postmistress Sees Flying Egg!

How to speak Alien: Expert breaks silence

I Flew to the Moon, Twice: Former alcoholic Clergyman takes the pledge

How to build your own alien shelter and what to wear in an alternate Universe

*Pictured: issue #19 of TUFOA magazine from June, 1997.
One article offered "How to build your own alien shelter
and what to wear in an alternate Universe."
The lead story referred to one of the first acts of Prime Minister Tony
Blair, elected in May 1997. Unfortunately for TUFOA, a rather
dim correspondent had misinterpreted a proposal from No 10
to relocate some recent foreign immigrants to special "holding"
accommodation in Chippenham, instead ascribing it to extraterrestrials.
Also the No 10 referred to in the article was actually No 10 Wiffle
Street, Malmsbury, the home of a local rhubarb grower anxious
to extend his workforce on the cheap.*

An early drawing by Adelbald shows his youthful interest in aliens.
The image was apparently created on a rainy Tuesday in a school
exercise book whilst the 11-year-old was supposedly taking
geometry lessons at St Cueball's Secondary, Hinge.
His headmaster chided him for inattention at the time and made
him stand in the corner of the classroom, his ankles immersed
in a cold soufflé, wearing the slogan "I must not draw
rubbish in class." As a result of this cruel act, Adelbald drew
nothing again... until he got home at 4pm, that is.

PART ONE

THE CASES

An alien creature photographed in the allotment
of retired fishmonger Delvis Bloom in the Westcountry
village of Codge, near Cobble, on the Cackhand borders.
Though a plague of similar creatures caused "havoc"
in the area, Bloom praised his own visitor for trimming his
Hollyhocks and weeding his fish pond before
transforming into a pikelet.

"The UFO is little more than a responsive, multi-generational transition from an Earth Mother fervour to an iconoclastic cosmic womb parallel where rationale is being impelled and coerced through the architecture of systemised programming. For every saucer there is a smudge on the lens; for every half wit there is a wit. Advice! Better spend your time planting rhubarb to seek the incremental balance between potting and potty. Even so, last week I saw a cigar-shaped craft hovering (or was it Hoovering?) in the shrubbery."

Neurologist Ben Trepanning, in his book *The Man Who Mistook His Wife for a Chamber Pot.*

First Things!

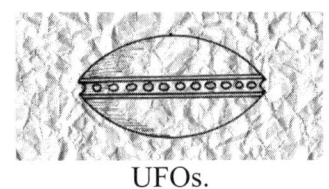

UFOs.

Unidentified Flying Objects.

Space ships packed with intergalactic travellers or just metallic doughnuts?
Are they with us now?
Have they always been with us?
Where are they from?
What do they want?
Are they real?
Are you likely to see one?
Do they always travel in pairs?
Are they really dangerous?
Should you welcome them into your back yard or just throw rocks at them?

We have no idea; we can only present the evidence.
There follow some intriguing case histories.

*The crumpled line illustration at the top of the page is by Staffordshire
potter Wilf Woolcast who spotted the sketched object hovering
over a village duck pond and "sucking up the goldfish
in a yellow beam of light." After making his drawing on the
back of an old parking ticket, Woolcast rushed home to
get his camera, but by the time he returned
two weeks later the "craft" had gone.*

Encounters!

Roadnap!

At 5.48am on 23 March, 1976, roof tile salesman Ed Clatter and retail chemist Jim Scrawn were separately driving along the Reno to Sacramento highway in California when the engines of their pickups mysteriously cut out, along with those of three other vehicles on the same stretch of road.

It was only minutes before they saw an eerie blue light, a giant silver saucer descended from the clouds and men wearing strange grey overalls approached each driver and handed him a business card recommending a high quality repair and breakdown service.

After checking everyone's oil and tyres and wiping their windshields the strangers departed in a cloud of smoke.

Balls!

A similar story is told by Oklahoma farmer Richard Delaware. He was calmly ploughing one of his 17-acre fields that same month when a large object fell from the sky with a crash.

At first he thought it was a refrigerator and continued ploughing. But when, at the end of the day, his wife told him that refrigerators did not fly he returned to the scene to investigate.

He found two silver spheres the size of a small refuse cart with a 3ft high being squatting beside them.

The being was naked except for boxer shorts, had a curious yellow skin speckled with orange polka-dots and was attempting to play Trivial Pursuit with Richard's tractor.

When Richard hailed the creature it leapt to its feet, which were webbed, and (through telepathy) demanded to see his income tax returns and a recipe for junket.

While he was walking back to his farmhouse to get them, Richard heard a whoosh and when he turned back, creature and craft and tractor had disappeared.

Dog-heist!

Another American farmer, John Owensborough, coincidentally the Mayor of a small mid-west town, was also visited by aliens one fall evening in 1977. He was confronted near his chicken house by a pink quadruped with frog-like eyes wearing a stovepipe hat and full evening dress. In a high-pitched shriek the creature told John in broken English that it was friendly and only wanted to take his dog, but became petulant when John offered his wife instead. In a fit of pique the creature showered John with a fine dust before it departed. The dust washed off easily and made many multi-coloured bubbles but was later discovered to be washing powder.

Planted!

English botanist Martin McGrady was astonished when answering a knock at his front door one evening in 1982 to find a 2ft high shrub-like being with a single stalked eye and carrying a hurricane lamp standing on his porch. The creature, which was predominantly green and covered with a variety of leaves and lichen, bleeped incessantly at McGrady who was swift to deduce that it was attempting to communicate in Morse.

A part-time coast guard, McGrady rapidly decoded the message which told him his floral visitor was on its way to a nearby vegetable show to seek out relatives and was both hungry and thirsty after its 500 million mile flight. McGrady allowed it to rest for an hour in his greenhouse, then sent it on its way with pruning shears and some Baby Bio. Its craft, he claims, was shaped like a geranium.

Hoax?
Hallucination?
Misidentification?
Insanity?

Perhaps...

Yet so many landings and contacts have taken place throughout the globe in the last century alone that it is no longer easy to dismiss the stories, many of which have their basis in FACT.

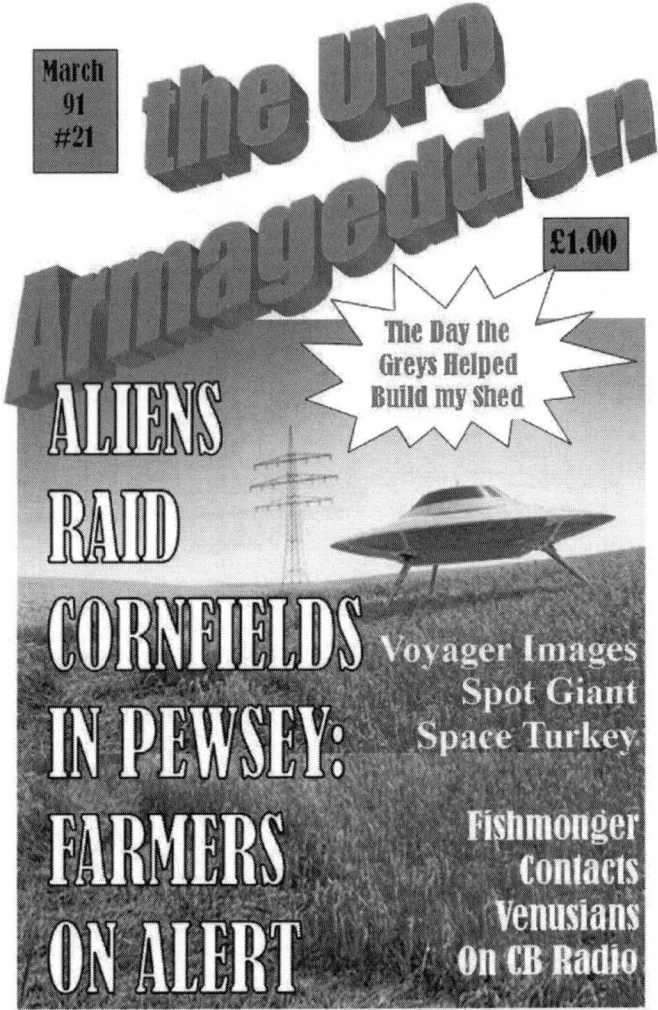

March 91 #21

the UFO Armageddon

£1.00

The Day the Greys Helped Build my Shed

ALIENS RAID CORNFIELDS IN PEWSEY: FARMERS ON ALERT

Voyager Images Spot Giant Space Turkey

Fishmonger Contacts Venusians On CB Radio

Here the Slumps hit on a "local" story that caused subdued panic among cereal eaters. One land owner was so distressed at the thought of being "told what to do by Martians" that he changed from arable farming to raising llamas overnight. The stress of the incident gave him a stiff neck and he has never looked back.

Background!

What is a UFO?

A UFO, or "unidentified flying object," is an object, seen to be flying – or at least airborne, i.e. up in the sky, which is the blue-grey stuff over our heads – that cannot be identified as a conventional terrestrial air vehicle, cloud formation, pterodactyl swarm or wedge of Caerphilly. It is assumed to be non-terrestrial in origin – i.e. not of this planet (Earth). Many believe these objects are "piloted" by "other beings" and numerous descriptions of these aliens have been lodged in the extensive, bulky files of Ufology, with a few scribbled in the margins of public telephone directories.

What is Ufology?

Ufology (pronounced *you foe olly jee*, after the 1920s Anglo-Franco-Algonquian basketball player Hugh Faux Awlychee) is a contemporary word, or neologism, or logical statement of Neo (an important character in *The Matrix*). It is used to describe the *logy* of the UFO; this in itself derives from the Ancient Greek λογία (logia), meaning someone who logs, which explains why so many of those studying unidentified flying objects are qualified industrial tree fellers.

The term was first recorded as far back as 1949 when Dagbert C. Rumplepudding, a US military colonel and tiddlywinks master, created the word when faced with some "awkward letters" during the nail-biting final of a Joint Forces Scrabble Tournament by trying to slip in an anagram of his granddaughter's nick-name, "Goofy Lu."

How is a UFO propelled?

There are numerous theories here, including the suggestion that they are individually launched from a massive rubber band based somewhere in the Andromeda Nebula. But the most likely methods of propulsion either involve some form of anti-gravity procedure or an electro-magnetism management course and there's quite a lot of complicated technical talk about Einstein (only some of it suggesting that the popular theoretical physicist was actually an extraterrestrial). Coal, oil and raspberry syrup have all been ruled out as power sources due to their unsuitability in providing sufficient momentum to launch chunky objects into huge intergalactic leaps across billions of light centuries.

How did it all start?

A caveman, often referred to as Ugg (though there is no independent verification of his real name if, indeed, he had one), is thought to have been the first human being to describe a sky-born chariot through his meticulous cave "paintings." These works – more scratchings with rudimentary charcoal than actual Louvre-quality canvases – were created around 300,000 years ago in a cluster of ancient caves hidden in a North African wadi.

They were unearthed in 1972, when a Donegal fruit-picker stumbled across the emmental-like grotto during a fortnight's recreational archaeology break with Saga. The "Ugg-Wadi Tapestry," as it became known, appears to show four-legged aliens with snouts and antenna, rearing up, as if in some galactic trance, although the cynics have dismissed the images as "gazelles."

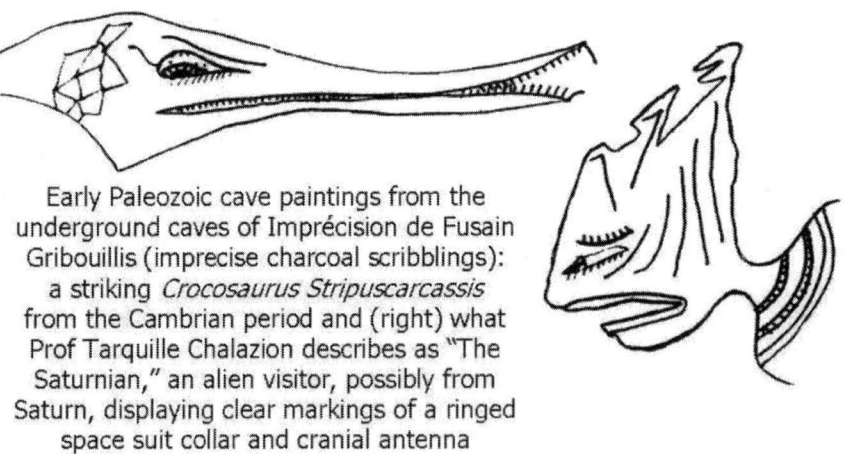

Early Paleozoic cave paintings from the underground caves of Imprécision de Fusain Gribouillis (imprecise charcoal scribblings): a striking *Crocosaurus Stripuscarcassis* from the Cambrian period and (right) what Prof Tarquille Chalazion describes as "The Saturnian," an alien visitor, possibly from Saturn, displaying clear markings of a ringed space suit collar and cranial antenna

Historic items from the Pierregritton Fine Art Collection

Taped!

Not all extraterrestrial visits have been friendly, as this transcript of an unexpurgated taped interview by writer Chappie Bonscatho with West Country housewife Norah Towling can attest!

Shelves!

MRS TOWLING

Well, I was out in the garden hanging up me washing. You know, the way I do every Thursday. Well, unless Jack – that's my husband – unless Jack's in the shed doing his shelf-making. Then it's a bit awkward hanging them up – my clothes that is – 'cause they drape in front of the shed window and cut out all his light and he gets in a bit of a fizz.

Anyway, as I said, I was just pinning his socks on the line when I heard this sort-of hum.

THE UFO ARMAGEDDON

Sort-of hum?

MRS TOWLING

Yes. Rather like a very very *very* large vacuum cleaner. And there was this light, which was rather surprising as it was three o'clock in the afternoon. It wasn't the sun because that'd just gone behind cousin Blanthorne's chimney and was throwing this big shadow over me peg bag.

Well, the next thing I knew was these two men, dressed in what looked like black plastic dustbin liners, were attaching these great hooks to the garage. And when I asked them what they was doing they said they was from the Gas Board, so I asked them if they'd like a cup of tea and when I came back out again with the cups they'd gone – and so had our garage!

I wouldn't mind, but it was packed full with me husband's book shelves. I mean, what's he going to say?

Just another trick of the light?
Just another bored housewife too keen on the cooking sherry?
We think not.

Norah Towling is a mainstay of the village community, a parish councillor and part-time lollypop lady (she makes the lollypops for Billy Sweetooth's Dorset Sweet Emporium). In her spare time she runs up crocheted winter slip-ons for pet chickens and is pictured below at a talk to her local W.I. on why she prefers dressing as a Victorian nanny whilst vacuuming the pantry.

Mrs Towling, photographed at the Webblihook Post Meridian Women's Institute's annual gas pipe renovation seminar where she won first prize in the fluff-disposal competition

Disguise!

How do aliens from another world hide themselves from us?

Experimental exobiologist Prof Dibden Smudge has speculated that many humanoid extraterrestrials have learned to cover themselves with a latex-style "skin" including false heads to simulate an Earth-dweller's appearance, as our illustration shows.

They use this "disguise" when collecting important biological samples, moving freely during fact-finding trips to populated areas, and to accommodate their work in various government and military installations, corporate businesses, communications networks, political offices and fairground fast food vans.

Smudge, who in his spare time weathers string to repel ectoplasm, says he once met a NASA scientist who claimed to have encountered a Belgian meat packer called Tom who swore that one of his co-workers was from *Triangulum Australe* and that his skin "moved." This was later dismissed when the elusive "Tom" was tracked down by journalists from a French welding magazine and found to be under the illusion that a popular antipodean continent was not as pictured in contemporary atlases but was "in reality" shaped like a "three-sided polygon." Tom's co-worker's skin moved, they added, when the rest of him moved, as when he walked across a room.

But can we trust their dismissive judgements?

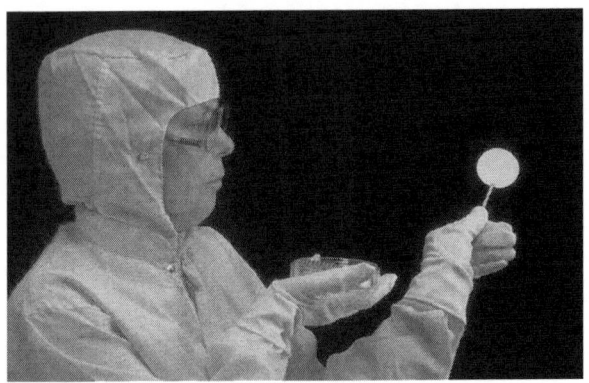

Prof Smudge is pictured with the "first lollypop on the moon," an apparently lemon-flavoured candy taken to the lunar surface in the lunar module by its lunar pilot Buzz "Lunar" Aldrin in his historic lunar visit of July 1969.

Smudge is testing the lollypop for traces of extraterrestrial DNA after an Aldrin fumble caused it to drop on to the moon's surface.

Fortunately, Aldrin managed to retrieve it from the ground during his unbroadcast speech "one awkward stretch for a man – oops, there goes my back."

From NASA's "contamination" archive

*An artist's impression of a smooth-skinned alien
with special "human" face mask and "adapted" hands.
It was spotted in a shopping centre in Buenos Aires in 1991.
When asked for directions to the headquarters of the
Policia Federal, the creature was alleged to have leapt into the
air, squeaked like a chipmunk and run off "at a speed
greater than a four-minute miler," thus suggesting
his potential extraterrestrial origins (or, perhaps,
a rather strident late night curry).
His clothes are off-the-peg modes from the
Javier Joaquin Gonzalo Valentin-Rodrigo and Jose Luis
Facundo Santiago-Leandro Fashion House, Bridlington.*

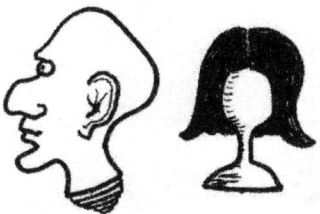

The kind of false head and false wig an alien might use.

The Harry Widdlescombe Chronicle!

Let's hear what happened to Norfolk butcher Harry Widdlescombe. *TUFOA* interviewed him for the regional television arts programme *On the Edge in Norfolk* and his story is recounted in full.

Harry is a soft-spoken man in his late fifties, well known locally for his huge facial warts which are often confused with his nose. He is a church sidesman and occasional juggler and has worked in the family butchery business since he was two.

Incident!

THE UFO ARMAGEDDON

Harry, could you tell us what you saw when you were stringing up the sausages on that fateful morning?

WIDDLESCOMBE (*transcript*)

Yes, well, I was in the shop and it was about ten past six. I start work about a quarter two and I was just stringing up the sausages and sorting out the offal for the day.

TUFOA

A difficult task?

WIDDLESCOMBE

Very. I like a good display in the window and I was just wiping down the shelves when I looked up.

TUFOA

This was the first time you realised something wasn't right?

WIDDLESCOMBE

Yes. The shelves were still dirty. While I was wiping them down I noticed a reflection in one of the marble slabs. Well, I turned and looked out over Wigginsville. You know Wigginsville? Well, my shop is right on top of the hill. There's only one hill in Wigginsville – pretty much the only big hill in Norfolk – and my shop is right on top of it, which is why I don't do a lot of trade these days as it's one in three and two miles up from the town centre...

TUFOA

A bit tough on the legs.

WIDDLESCOMBE

It is. Well, I looked out over Wigginsville and I saw this orange blob, sort-of hovering over the rooftops. I didn't know what it was. I thought it was something in the glass, a reflection, 'cause we've got this new KX5 meat shredder out the back, and that's got an orange light on it.

TUFOA

You immediately thought it was the KX?

WIDDLESCOMBE

Right. So I went outside to eliminate the reflection thing and it was still there. I watched it for quite a while, and I was still there when Ethel called me for my eight o'clock cuppa, so it must've been about two hours.

TUFOA

What did the light *do*?

WIDDLESCOMBE

For a long time it just hovered there and I thought it was a trick of perspective – an optical refraction, or something. Then all of a sudden it loomed in and came up over the house and shop and hung there like a big orange disk. It just glowed and pulsed like a great orange heart hanging there.

TUFOA

How did you feel?

WIDDLESCOMBE

I was shaking by this time, of course. Then it just shot out a light, and the light just came down into the road about ten feet away, and in the light there was this THING - like a man, but with far too many arms and legs. Probably about six or eight. And it said: "Good morning, Harry." Which I thought was very extraordinary for something like this. Then Ethel called me for my breakfast and I had to go in.

Harry the butcher, chairman of the Ancient Order of
Wigginsville and District Offallers

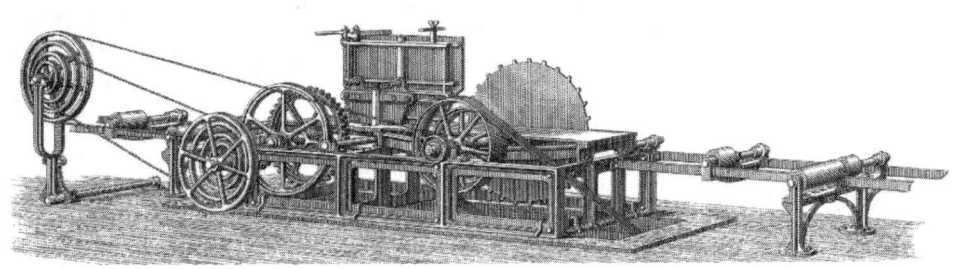

The KX5 Meat shredder Mk 1.7
Image courtesy of mechanical engineers
Hamilton, Sparbender and Ludge

Unanswered!

Questions!

Did spacemen give us the boiled egg, candlesticks and continental quilts?

Was the Brussels sprout the result of an alien cabbage experiment that went tragically wrong?

Was New Zealand once part of Italy?

Is our moon really an enormous cosmic golf ball?

Does a secret trans-galactic starship service really exist – and, if so, how difficult would it be to buy a return ticket to Ursa Minor?

These are just some of the many unanswered questions that lead us to the irrefutable fact that something is wrong with our history as we know it!

Ready to tee off?

Casefiles!

A 2,000-year-old precooked dinner for two, excavated at a secret ancient site in Asia.
Does this mean that early space visitors were outside caterers?

Blue and green striped rocks that yodel when kicked have been found in a New Guinea forest.
Gifts from the Space Gods?

A football boot, millions of years old, found in the Gobi Desert.
Signs of early team work between aliens and humans?

A 3,000-year-old Sanskrit codex that gives elaborate details on how to build an electric toaster.
Technology from the stars?

Three mummified merchant bankers found in a fifth-century archaeological dig at Cadbury, England.
No great loss?

All signs of so-called Astral Travellers?
We think so! Their legend has even spread into literature!

Books!

Could this Eastern document tell of a visit by spacemen?

El Khala Bala Falalla, Sixth-century mystic and hemp seller, records this:

"And lo, they did look into the sky
and they did see a cloud
and it did rain."

Here the SKY referred to is clearly an alien spacecraft, the CLOUD an opening hatchway and the RAIN spasmodic laser fire!

Renaissance poet Ludicrous Amiander wrote:

"Up into the starry sky you fly
Are you a bird, or not?"

In that extract from his renowned 23-volume *Seeings and Doings*, Amiander is clearly observing a flying saucer. If it had been a mere bird he would have named it!

Amiander is pictured *overleaf* in a woodcut by Jorgio Pagliacci holding a copy of the 19th volume of his epic work. It includes a discourse on the viability of crop rotation on a glacier, walking in moccasins made from lutes and the extent of the visible (and non-visible) galaxy as viewed from a very tall ladder roped to the roof of the Palazzo Montecitorio on a starry night in October 1652 (give a decade or two either way).

Ludicrous Amiander (or "chicken boy") in a woodcut by Jorgio Pagliacci, from the Adalberto Foggia collection

We have uncovered an astounding catalogue of MEN and THINGS visiting our world for purposes unknown. But what about women? Are there no ladies in Space? Yes, according to Venezuelan peasant Jose Valpeso!

Sex!

At 61, 19-stone Valpeso was abducted from his imported yak ranch and taken aboard a large spacecraft shaped, he claims, like a mutton chop. There he was intimately examined by a network of moving pipes and tubes then placed in a small lozenge-shaped chamber on his own. A beautiful woman with long, flowing golden hair and cat-like eyes entered the room and made love to him for three months. Then he was suddenly and unaccountably released to wander in the desert for two days until he found his way home, weighing just 112lbs. Valpeso never speaks of the incident now. He just wanders aimlessly around his home town, shuffling slightly, but never losing that wide-eyed stare and an even wider grin.

Not thought to be Valpeso

A Brief History!

Fighters!

The "flying cowpat" (later re-classified as "flying saucer" after the intervention of US censors) came into its own during World War Two when pilots described large and mysterious khaki blobs following their aircraft. These became known as Poo Fighters and led to the US Air Force setting up its own investigation of the phenomena through its exhaustive Project Poo Book.

Its cases echo comparable incidents from the previous century involving "phantom airships," "skittish balls of light" and attacks by "wild-eyed" buzzards armed with pilfered salt and pepper cruets. Many similar wartime occurrences are recorded as far back as the Roman Conquest of Somerset, England, when some of Caesar's crack legions reported being followed by clusters of flying turnips.

"Mayday, mayday – poo alert!"

Threat!

Most unqualified governments and sniffy academics naively believe these sightings are no threat to national security and continue to cling to the outmoded excuses that we are seeing clouds, weather balloons, the planet Venus, terrestrial aircraft, "buoyant plasma formations" or hedgehogs on trampolines. They say we just need our eyes tested!

But it is those GOVERNMENTS AND ACADEMICS that are SHORT-SIGHTED and not us, as our own meticulous research shows.

Survey!

A major survey into aerial phenomena held by the Bedruthany-Chameleon Astronomical Society in 1989 had a positive return of 98% from 22,000 responding members of the public.

However, the society was forced to repeat the exercise after it was felt that the single question "Have you ever seen anything in the sky?" was a little too broad.

A revised survey, with the question "Have you ever seen anything in the sky that you cannot identify?" received the following response: 62% Yes, 21% No, 8% Don't Know and 9% Liberal Democrats.

Identify!

There are six categories of UFO classification under the provisos of the Helsinki Optimum Procedure of Phenomena Identification & Notification Gradation (HOPPING).

1 Up-There Lights (Mostly night)
2 Up-There Lumpy Things (Mostly day)
3 Probably Up-There, Not Sure (radar, sonar, cumulonimbus, fluff)
4 Up-There, But Missed It Myself, Sorry (snapshots, reflections in mirrors/windows/partner's eyes/ponds, etcetera)
5 Shook Hands With Them (inter-species contact made)
6 Liberal Democrats

Somerset saucer leaves telltale landing marks!

Somerset television executive and amateur fruit bottler Edland de Paull Trank was "taking the air" on a quiet hillside close to his country home one sunny afternoon in August 1991 when he heard an unusual noise coming from the far side of a high hedge. Startled, yet mysteriously drawn to explore the phenomenon, the energetic 36-year-old scrambled up the incline, apparently to the sound of "two steam trains grinding over a concrete causeway littered with metal shavings, broken bottles and popcorn." He arrived to see a disappearing shape in the sky, which he guessed was the source of the disturbance, and was quick to aim his

Panjandrum 4 – a collectable and still serviceable Polaroid camera left to him in the will of a late Victorian aunt – to take this clear and unambiguous record of an alien visitation.

The circular depression left on the ground by the previously-landed and fast-departing craft is clearly visible across the bottom of the picture, as is a wide "path-like" depression in the bottom centre of the shot caused by the "exhaust" backdraft of the saucer as it rapidly left the area on detecting a human's approach.

A detailed investigation of the area by UFOA freelance investigator Arlan Pittlespan showed clear signs of disturbance, and a subsequent chemical analysis of a half pint of soil from the "exhaust" depression revealed traces of various carbons, mucus, bovine and Lagomorhpa (rabbit) digestive matter, dandruff, wheat shucks and a rare kind of draper's sausage*.

Pittlespan also says he detected traces of an unidentifiable "fuel" which he claimed was "mislaid" during analysis by his local chemist.

*A small band of West Country drapers became renowned during a seventies butchers' strike for illegally making their own sausages to aid selected locals starved of the meaty treat, secretly wrapping them in small tea towels, table napkins or cake doilies with a cautious wink and a small additional payment (ranging from several pence to as much as £3 for a full 1lb strand).

The Extraordinary Pipp and Blake Interview!

Apart from the many sightings of Unidentified Flying Objects recorded on ancient cave walls, in mediaeval paintings and on modern plastic toilet seats there have also been numerous encounters by the FAMOUS: Winston Churchill, Alexander the Great, King Arthur, Joan of Arc, Davy Crockett and top international journalist Maggie Pipp and fashion photographer Hettie Blake.

In this extract from an interview in *BUXOM*, the clothes magazine for girls with the fuller figure, the women outline their spooky experience.

BUXOM MAGAZINE

Maggie, you interviewed artist Dalvador Saali in a rubber pigeon loft just after he'd turned down a commission from the Imaginary Pope Norbert the Second to re-paint the Sistine Chapel. And Hettie, you photographed dancer Wayne Slope in a tricky routine with a troupe of fifteen animated toucans all dressed as Fred Astaire. But have either of you ever had any really *strange* encounters in your careers?

MAGGIE PIPP

Yes! It was a night in April, 1988. I'd been reviewing Lax Pendleton's *Androgynous* at the Barbican for the May edition of *Exotic Eroticus* and Hettie had been photographing the innovative new Snoit collection of latticed bustiers at Fellipi's fashionable Kensington restaurant Crepes Touché. It had been a long day, obviously, and we were out on the rooftop patio at Hettie's Hampstead apartment in the Jacuzzi, just relaxing and thumbing through the spring edition of *Great Hungarian Poncho Designs*, when we heard this deafening noise.

HETTIE BLAKE

Deafening! It sent all these ripples across the water. Loads more than those from Maggie's intestinal problems.

PIPP

It was a whirring sound, rather like a huge washing machine.

BLAKE

But with no clothes in it.

PIPP

So we leapt out of the tub and there was this bright light shining on the decking, like a West End stage spotlight or an arc light at Wembley for the Cup Final. Not that I watch football, obviously.

BLAKE

But you like the players.

PIPP

Mmm. And there was this mist and then this shape: long and semi-oval, like a cigar. And there was this ladder that seemed to drop down from nowhere. It was one of those galvanised type of ladders...

BLAKE

You see them in Texas.

PIPP

I've never been to Texas.

BLAKE

Or B&Q...

PIPP

Oh. And this sort-of man came down the rungs wearing a sort-of Bakofoil suit and a strange hat, sort-of head-shaped. And there was this sort-of glass panel in the front of the suit, rather like a microwave oven.

BLAKE

There was nothing cooking, though.

PIPP

And he started walking towards us. Well, by this time the mist was making everything go cold and we became aware that we were standing there all wet and completely naked.

                    BLAKE

Except for the towels.

                    PIPP

Except for the towels, yes.

                    BLAKE

And the goose bumps.

                    PIPP

And we were starting to get a bit worried. You know, two semi-naked women in the middle of nowhere...

                BUXOM MAGAZINE

In the middle of Hampstead.

                    PIPP

It was very late! Two women alone, no-one around, with an enormous flying machine full of spacemen hovering overhead; not knowing what they were going to do, if their intentions were honourable.

                    BLAKE

You were grinning.

                    PIPP

It was fear! Anyway, this man, this being, walked slowly over to us and I could see he was holding out this little white tube about three to four inches long. Well, we thought it was a ray gun, you know, like you do, and we were about to run when he opened a door in his hat, or helmet, put the tube in his mouth and said: "*Have you got a light, girls?*"

                    BLAKE

I can still hear it now, plain as the face on her nose.

Maggie and Hettie talk bubbly...

WOW! It goes right up your nose, doesn't it,
darling.
Hettie and yours truly true, Maggie Pipp have just come back to Blighty from a *fabulosa* trip to the
champagne region of Touts a-la Bec de-Truffules in Lower Normandy and we were legless for much

The dynamic duo feature in the collectors' magazine Fine Wines and Flatulence

Promotion

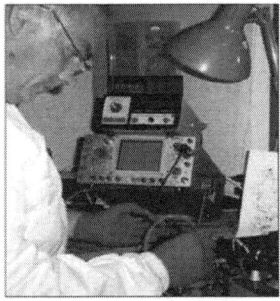

Moor aliens!

The Slumps helped finance the publication of a rare "local" book set in Devon, *Aliens Over Dartmoor*, written and researched by the reclusive retired toenail consultant J. Crockett-Baunder. The book is now so rare that prominent international manuscript vendor *Rare Books, Birdcages, Accordion Music and Player Piano Rolls* has the only traceable copy of the 52-page soft cover volume from the mid-seventies.

Aliens Over Dartmoor

An authoritative account
by

J. Crockett-Baunder, M.D.

RBBAMPPR states in its Autumn catalogue that the book is: "Pretty Good, second hand (possibly third but no more than 16th), no dust jacket (as it's a paperback, you doofus), spine firm (but buttocks flabby), some rubbing of the corners (and gentle stroking of the edges), a little foxing with a trace of badger. SIGNED (but only by one of Dr Baunder's patients)."

Crockett-Baunder never allowed himself to be photographed during his lifetime, although he did permit a local artist to paint him in his living room on the understanding that he (Crocket-Baunder) remained obscured behind a bookcase. Following the disbursement of Baunder's will, the painting sold for £3 in an Okehampton charity shop auction and has since disappeared (possibly during Bonfire Night).

Here are some of the extraordinary stories recorded by the author in his delvings.

The Abduction of Snuffles. How a Yelverton sheepdog was whisked away by an unknown sky craft in the late fifties and returned 20 years later with extraordinary skills. Snuffles became fluent in three languages, ate with a knife and fork and bought a villa in Nice with the proceeds of his appearance on the popular television show *You Clever Dog!*

Cattle Sprucing. The strange experiences of lifelong dairyman George Graddlehonker, who reports that on at least five occasions his Friesian herd was sucked aboard "a girt big saucer-like thing" and returned hours later with their fur coiffured and their horns and hooves waxed as if for an agricultural show.

My Dog! Tells the tail (sic) of a Tiverton hairdresser who claimed she had an astral affair with a blonde-skinned being from "Ultratopia Magnus" who called himself "Bunny" and shaved only his toes. He took her to the Dog Star and she came back with a puppy.

In *I Speak to the Atlantians*, Baunder writes of the exclusive Agaricus Institute and its cryptic leader Bill Pelmet, a former holiday camp coach driver who claimed to have encountered the Angel Gabriel on a ferris wheel in Shrewsbury. Pelmet maintains he has an "open link" to an alien leader called Datura, one of the original Atlanteans, who speaks to him in a string of electrical impulses which Pelmet deciphers through elaborate dance movements. These kicks, turns and taps are then interpreted into modern English by his close collaborator Moonstalker Prime (part-time garden landscaper Zoe Tramshaft) and re-translated into runic script by group mapmaker and graphologist Burgundy Fungus, just to show off.

In *The Insolent Spectre of Poddlecombe Cross*, we learn of the ghostly image of a twelfth-century monk who appears each Maundy Thursday at around 9pm in a reedy upland coppice taunting passers-by with his tongue out and sneaking up on those with their backs turned and pinching their bottoms. One distressed visitor was quoted as saying: "It had my bottom pinched. It was horrible. I don't know what I'm going to do without it."

In *Hollow Tors*, writer Beth Stewd-Lentil speculates that several remote tors may hide terrestrial bases for at least one space-travelling race. She cites testimony from several moor hikers and "letterboxers" who have heard a curious underground knocking emanating from these important mounds in the dead of night; one even claimed he had knocked on the side of such a hillock and received three return knocks, at which point he ran away. Tam Widdler's *Old map of Dartmoor* shows the entrances to three supposed alien bunkers along with the sites of several underground forests.

Other thought-provoking articles include *The Smirking Clown of Great Monkey Tor*, the story of a puzzling outcrop which, like the famous face of Mars, can only be seen from the air with the sun in the right position and only after tiffin; and *The Coal Black Chicken of Hameldown Beacon*, a phantom hen said, if seen, to impart bad luck to the viewer, much like the ghostly canine of British folklore; the curse is worse should the chicken lay a black egg, especially if the egg is taken away and used in an omelette as a gripey stomach usually ensues.

Unconfirmed!

Letter!

Former Wing-Cdr Nobby "Nobs" Knobbington, occupant of Room 13 of the Elijah Pertinent Home for the Psychedelically Unhinged, Witherfone, Dorset, writes:

Sir,

I was based at RAF Tangle-Blastit in the mid-1960s and the Air Ministry had just launched the UK's own formal UFO enquiry, Project Red, White and Blue Book. *The first time that I caught a glimpse of something "not of this Earth" was on a spring Sunday when I was out on the runway with Binky, Bonky, Chippie, Choppy and Chirpy having a quick ruck in a game of three-a-side rugger.*

Old Chippie went for an impossible tackle and ended up flat on his back between my legs and pointing. Well, I thought the old truss had come undone, then I heard Binky shouting, turned round and there it was: about 20ft over our heads, silver colour, apparently circular, big dome at the top, and these enormous tentacles. Biggest flying jellyfish I've ever seen – and I've seen a few things like that in my time in the cockpit! Well, we had to stop the game; one of us might have been stung.

Anyway, Bonky went for a net and some skin cream and by the time he got back it had shut itself in a hanger and was refusing to come out. We never saw it again, but that may be because we all left immediately for Malaya.

Tecchano!

Most lads with a bent for model making will have owned a Tecchano set at some time. But how many remember the infamous Tecchano Set 41, *Build Your Own Flying Saucer*, a kit with metal strips, nuts and bolts, moulded fibreglass panels, Perspex domes, fibre optic cabling and various adhesive hydrocarbon secretions; remember finally enveloping the completed machine in an airtight tarpaulin skin? Very few, because it was suppressed within hours of being released! The schematics for the craft were said to have been stolen from the MOD, though most Sixties scooter riders deny this.

A clue to the existence of the much-denied Set 41 is confirmed by Tecchano's use of the numeral itself. For 41 is the number of seconds involved in the motion of stars known as an "aberration" (an unmistakable outer space connection) and is also the age of the world's oldest-recorded living goldfish – a cunning reference to the giant but elusive omnivorous *plasma fantail* of Cassiopeiae 10, said to have been photographed by Voyager 2, though the pictures were never developed.

Artist's impression of the "missing" Set 41

Vanished!

The Prevost/Van Hool Experiment was a notorious incident in which two Greater Manchester buses vanished from their routes around Wardley and Crumpsall on a dreary Thursday in 1984, only to reappear 5,000 miles away and two weeks earlier in Guatemala in the middle of the Semana Santa religious festival. The episode caused both outrage and consternation, especially amongst those passengers who only had tickets to Urmston.

Each coach was rumoured to have been involved in a secret military trial aimed at "cloaking" the vehicles, where scientists employed both magnetic fields and free-particle spaghetti mounds to render the vehicles invisible during times of danger, such as wartime or whenever they were approached by a teenager. Bus personnel and passengers were returned safely and, despite being covered in a liberal dusting of sawdust and flower petals, claimed no memory of the incident, insisting instead that they had only been to the Kirkgate Shopping Centre in Bradford.

Fate!

Contemporary extraterrestrial archaeologist and international baboon importer Henri Parsley Doppelganger tells of the pan-galactic fate of planes, boats and rhubarb stalks lured to oblivion in the Lake Windermere Triangle.

He recounts the strange markings in the sand at Nazca, Peru which closely resemble the internal mechanism of a modern pin ball machine.

He also highlights
the fabulous ancient map of Blind Hucca-Hucca, drawn in 1412, or at nearly a quarter past two, where skilled, apparently AERIAL cartography accurately shows the coast of Switzerland before it became land-locked,
the Great Well of China (the biggest natural hole ever seen),
and a future motorway service station car park on the M25.

*H.P. Doppelganger, pictured after a Botox weekend
on the Isle of Wight*

Doppelganger even records the most famous alien crash story in UFO literature, where at least one craft is said to have plunged to Earth and several alien bodies were recovered and hidden from the public: the great Boswell Incident of 1773.

The Great Boswell Incident!

Crash!

Renowned Scottish writer and lawyer James Boswell was taking a tour of the Hebrides with Dr Samuel Johnson that year, 1773. Boswell witnessed the now-historic UFO incident at a local sheep farm shortly after a visit to Sir Allan Macnoggie, chief of the Macnoggie clan and 6th Baronet of Twill, who was known to make an outstanding haggis-and-kedgeree bake. What Boswell experienced is still contentious, even today.

Boswell wrote in his journal that he saw a smashed saucer-shaped "flying stagecoach" with several grey beings scattered around it and even got to suck on a piece of metal from the crash, which he claimed tasted "minty."

Before he could investigate further the local militia sealed off the area, took both the pieces of the craft and its occupants away on several ox carts for analysis at a mainland cavalry headquarters and all evidence vanished.

Boswell petitioned Parliament for the truth to be known, but only the King believed him, and as George III was himself deemed "sixpence short of a halfpenny" the tale passed into legend, then analytical obscurity.

Boswell was a believer!

Already bearing the burden of a background of Catholicism, comic songs, mistresses and genital ague, Boswell was ridiculed and only regained his stature by penning a string of articles for the London Magazine, none of which alluded to alien invasion.

Johnson, who was half blind, half deaf and for some unaccountable reason hated Americans, was so distressed by the experience that he retired to his bed for eight years to compose a 40,000-word dictionary which SIGNIFICANTLY excluded the word SPACEMEN. Undoubtedly both men were silenced.

At the time, Boswell's friend Voltaire commented that "if aliens did not exist it would be necessary to invent them" and Rousseau, with whose mistress Boswell had instigated a boisterous affair, commented: "Aliens are born free, yet here they are in chains. Oy! Get back in the house, Therese; I know where you're off to, you *mechant* slapper!"

Stories of the Boswell crash continue to resound throughout UFO sources even today and there is even a small cafe on a hillock in Skye which offers Spacebeing Pie, Warminster Waffles, Yoofo Buns and the popular lunchtime special Adamski's Hot Stew with Zamora dumplings.

Choose your own dish
(Sandwich board from Sloppy Signs Ltd)

Other Things!

Bridge!

The man who exploited Voyager fly-by snaps to discover the controversial Ear of Venus, scientist Gentian Hasselblatt III, now claims evidence for a giant primeval space bridge between Jupiter and Saturn. He says that confirmation has come from previously-suppressed NASA probe photographs which clearly show debris in an asteroid belt between the two planets containing ice, breeze blocks, twisted steel girders and a pair of backhoe loaders.

More!

Retired astronomer Hollis Detrellian Thetaparticle, who spent a lifetime plotting the luminosity and temperature of distant stars only to discover that the pivotal Hertzsprung-Russell Diagram was merely a quick sketch on the bottom of a table mat, joins the debate. He posits that:

Aliens who built the giant stone dolls of Easter Island did so to advertise their trade in giant stone hats!

The great city of Machu Picchu was built high in the Andes Mountains by space visitors anxious to avoid early Peruvian insurance salesmen!

French Emperor Napoleon once passed through a spatial displacement vortex near Santiago de Compostela during his invasion of Portugal in 1807 which subsequently caused his hairpiece to spontaneously rise from his scalp and rotate at least twice a day until his death. This led to the 19th Century saying: "That's as plausible as a spin on Bonaparte's Wig."

"Zee glue is only a temporary solution..."

Before the lost lands of Atlantis, Mu and Gondwana became swamped by unfriendly tides, there was another world yet to be unaccounted for. The sparsely-translated *Chronicles of Di'HanyQin* record the existence of antediluvian clay tablets containing legends of the Hidden Plateau of Oggiola del Oggi – "north-west of the Far-Reaching Doldrums of Tsush, but not as far as the Prodigious Depression of Mnmpf" – where it is recorded that the huge mullet-smoking chimneys of Huun became the bedrock pillars for the Exalted Temple of Yiy, wherein was worshipped the Great Bod, "and woe betide any passing traveller wielding the Mallet of Stains."

Machu Picchu, the ancient Peruvian site and popular tourist trap,
is being brought into the modern age.
Plans exist for a cluster of twelve five-storey holiday
apartment blocks with "the view to die for – which
you will do if you drop off the edge..."

The Historic Thorn Starchild Radio Broadcast!

Serial!

The problem is, mainstream science fiction has distorted the facts – even more than the military! Take, for example, this late 1940s UK-US radio serial, *Thorn Starchild, Space Cadet!*

TONIGHT ON
THE HOME
SERVICE AT 7.30PM

"Radio Times and Tides" magazine programme notification from 1951

This extract was transcribed in the UFO-sceptic magazine *Flying Saucers are Daft* and reproduced by *The UFO Armageddon* without permission because we don't like them.

FX: Strident music, background ray gun fire, lots of Americans shouting.

GUARD
Captain Zob! Captain Zob! The evil Emperor Fang and the Zorg people are attacking the city!

CAPT ZOB
What?! Summon our galactic hero Jetpack Kewchin immediately! He and his amazing positron ray will dispatch these foul fiends swiftly.

GUARD

But Captain Zob, Jetpack was caught in a powerful time-warp spiral by the nefarious Thong of Grath in episode three. We are defenceless!

CAPT ZOB

Wait! There is another who can help us! Gallant, intrepid, valiant, brave, undaunted and bold! None other than blond, smart and handsome rocket pilot Thorn Starchild, Space Cadet!

FX: Laboratory sounds.

DERRY PINKHAM

Oh, Thorn, I so admire you! Your handsome looks, your flowing red cape and boots and that skin-tight lime green body stocking. Come away from your machines for a moment and hold me close.

THORN STARCHILD

Sorry, Derry, but I've important work here. I have to reassemble this hoop-and-twizzle zap gun left behind by Doctor Andron when he was turned into a cheese in episode one. I don't have time for his pretty assistant Derry Pinkham - even if you are a real woman with real flesh and blood, a very skimpy costume and first class lumpy bits.

INTERCOM

Emergency, emergency! Space Cadet Starchild to Omicron leader Captain Zob at Battle Station Alpha. Urgent you destroy Emperor Fang and the Zorgs before Utopia City is obliterated!

THORN

Great guns, Derry, they need me! I must save the world! Look after things here. I'll be back in, ooh, twenty minutes.

ANNOUNCER

Meanwhile, far away...

FANG

So! They dare to bring in space cadet Thorn, eh? I, Emperor Fang, will see to it that those feeble heroes of Utopia City are totally smashed. Bodyguard Mung! Prime and load the dreaded sheep ray. Ha ha ha. That will be the end of Captain Zob and his foolish followers. Fire!

FX: Whoosh! followed by running sounds.

DERRY

But I've told you, Thorn, I'm coming with you. I love you and I want to be beside you when you fight the evil Zorgs.

THORN

All right, Derry. But please let go of my shorts, it's slowing us down as we race down this corridor to avert further disaster.

FX: Whooshing sound.

THORN

Wait! What's that? That terrible light and that noise in my head. Argh!

DERRY

Argh!

FX: Whooshing reaches crescendo and dies off.

THORN
(*sounding like a sheep*)

Whaaat on Eaaarth waaas thaaat?

DERRY
(*likewise*)

Whaaat's haaappened to yooour voiiiice?

THORN

Nooo! Emperooor Faaang haaas releeeased his dreeeaded sheeeep raaay!

CAPT ZOB

Thorrrn, Thorrrn! This is dreeeadful. Evvveryone in Utopiaaa City is taaalking like Laaarry the Laaamb!*

ANNOUNCER

A 1930s radio favourite...

THORN

Caaaptain, it's traaagic!

DERRY

I caaan't go on like this forrr the rest of my liiife, Thorrrn. I'm a beauuutiful womaaan. How caaan I go on with a voiiice like thiiis, and waaalking about on aaall fourrrs?

DR ANDRON

Well, at leeeast yourrr not a cheeeeese!

ALL

Shuuut uuup, Dr Andronnn!

FANG

Mung, it's dreaaadful, the sheeep raaay haaas baaackfired and the Zorrrgs are aaall taaalking like this tooooo!

MUNG

It's reeealy baaaaaaaad luck!

No, that kind of fictional rubbish doesn't help the devotee at all. It makes us UFO buffs, who see spacemen behind every hill and bush during every hour of the day and night, seem like demented penguins. Yet there are still disbelievers.

Popular character from historic BBC children's programme Toytown

TV Comes Up Trumps!

Jammy!

Here's another UFO heretic, Professor Champion de Vunderhause, who gets his comeuppance in a rare, hard-to-find recording of the one-off Yorkshire television show *Are You a Sceptic?* which proves, once again, that TRUTH will always be stranger than FICTION!

After a string of interviews with anti-UFO lobbyists, here's what the Welsh professor of student architecture told the programme's presenter Jimmy James Jammy on that fateful afternoon in 1973 at the climax of proceedings: "This whole spaceman business is a load of utter twaddle, nonsense, bilge, poppycock, trash, absurdity, foolishness, stupidity and piffle."

Jammy responded, "So, you don't give the idea of alien life much credence, then?" Vunderhause said no and his wife Plantagena and his two children Desmond and Dorothy agreed. At this point, Jammy made a revelation. According to this tape source, which has been vilified by numerous sources as fake but confirmed by the Southern Provinces Gas Board as genuine footage, Jammy then said he would like to surprise Vunderhause. Jammy moved to a huge green velvet curtain that divided the stage, the Vunderhause family, a small technical crew and the fifty-strong studio audience from the back of the auditorium.

Jammy spoke, pulling no punches for the UFO community. To an accompanying pre-recorded drum roll, he told Prof Vunderhause, "Right behind that curtain is tonight's Star Prize on *Are You a Sceptic?* And it is your own disbelieving attitude and complete disregard for the evidence presented to you tonight that has won you the top trophy!"

Mrs Vunderhause piped up, "Is it a car? I've always wanted a car, haven't I, children?"

The children said they preferred a holiday at Disneyland, but the Professor just clipped their ears and they began crying. At this point the presenter called his assistant, a strawberry blonde dressed in a red glitter swim suit and fireman's helmet, to tug on a rope and pull back the huge green curtain. Jammy told them their prize wasn't a car and the audience gasped as the curtain parted to reveal a silver flying saucer, the size of a small bungalow, with an open hatchway and ramp. Then the true nature of the incident revealed itself.

Jammy told them, "This is the real thing! An inter-spatial, inter-dimensional craft! Capable of wonders. And the tedious Vunderhause family has won a two week trip around the Solar System, starting immediately, with me as their pilot and host. Let me slip off this mask and introduce myself."

The audience went "Oooh" and Jammy tugged at the side of his head peeling back a latex human face to reveal a green scaly skin, two small antennas, red eyes and several leafy protrusions from around his thick neck. In a deep, sonorous voice he said, "*My name is Qua-Qua. I come from the Sirius star system. Our planet greets you. Step aboard, insignificant humans.*"

Jammy (or "Qua-Qua") and his lovely assistant Bubbles ("Bubbles") ushered the dumbstruck family into the craft and, just before the door closed behind them, he turned to the now panic-stricken audience. He laughed and said, "*That's what you get for not believing. See you on the highway some night.*" He waved, slammed the hatch and the craft took off and vanished through a skylight in the studio roof.

Jimmy James Jammy and the Vunderhause Family (latterly chosen as the name for a popular Bluegrass revival group) have not been heard of since that terrifying broadcast.

The authorities deny it ever happened. They claim the tape is a forgery. They say the people shown are actors on a bogus set. They have produced "evidence" that the broadcast never took place.

Even *The UFO Armageddon* has been unable to track down any of the "audience" that allegedly attended the recording, a grainy VHS copy of which is in our possession.

But we all know what happens to people who have seen too much...

Finally!

We all know how easy it is to "disappear" people.

How simple it is to HIDE THE TRUTH when Governments conspire to SUPPRESS it.

How gullible we all can be when faced with the stark choice between WHAT WE KNOW and THE CONVENTIONAL, ACCEPTED and ACCEPTABLE view.

How hard it is to live with the stain of being dubbed a SOCIAL OUTCAST, ECCENTRIC or a simple WEIRDO-NUT LOONYBONCE!

But *The UFO Armageddon* can only say this: Keep an open mind.

Keep clear of dangerous mental whitewash.

Change your underwear frequently and never wear a conch shell on your head.

Entertainment!

Most importantly, reflect on the hidden messages behind these words from vital, challenging and INDEPENDENT Science Fiction entertainment…

"Gort! Klaatu barada nikto! Nikto, Montgomery, nikto! Jubjub trolli kazoo."

… the non-literal translation of which is: My rubber tubing has been stencilled with hexagons.

This may be a somewhat obtuse statement, but nonetheless it is comforting in its own particular way.

And who could disagree?

In conclusion, here's an essential appeal, its veracity confirmed by poet and pitch steamer Daniel B. Handtowel in an address to the Quench Academy Forum, Massachusetts in 1981. He advised delegates to

Footnote!

The chief researcher for *The UFO Armageddon* magazine between 1991 and 1997 was journalist, broadcaster, writer and musician Chappie "Off Road" Bonscatho, a long-time friend of the Slumps and a man whose devotion to stockpiling UFO literature was so great that he referred to his collection of books, periodicals and papers by magnitude, as in: "I have more than 23 tons of that, thank you."

He kept most of his revered collection in a garden shed but was latterly unable to reference any of it as he found it impossible to open the door.

His globe-trotting led to a first encounter with an Unidentified Flying Object in 1971 when a large white craft shaped like a potato chased him through the outskirts of Genoa at 3am after a concert of mediaeval lute music. When he encountered a cluster of silver saucers on a cycling holiday in Kent the following year, he began researching the phenomenon.

Around this time he met Australian immigrant John "Billabong" Pinker who taught him how to play the didgeridoo (a long tubular Antipodean wind instrument) and gave him his nick-name "Off Road" due to his inability to ride a bicycle in a straight line.

In the last twenty years of his life Chappie allegedly investigated more than 100 million UFO cases, from sightings to abductions and, aside from his articles for *UFO Armageddon*, wrote 23 books on the subject, including *Spaceships from Space, The Cosmic Plant Invasion (Whoosh! It's in a Bush), What's That Up There, Doc?* and the monster-selling *They Lived On Riga 3: Life With the Hydrogen Wedges*.

Chappie moved from newspapers and magazines to television in 1979. He specialised in dog shows, golden weddings and winkle-picking galas. He was eaten alive by topiary in 2002.

Chappie Bonscatho – as always, dressed in his best explorer's gear – watches out for saucers in a secret rural UFO hot spot in West Cornwall during a pisky baiting weekend.
(Picture: The Polpenweadle Pasty Times)

PART TWO

THE MAGAZINE

MONSTERS FROM THE COSMOS DESCEND ON HAMPSHIRE VILLAGE: CAUSE CHAOS

More than twenty sightings of strange creatures from another star system have taken place in the tiny village of Codge, the former home of popular county cricketer Billy "Wack-em" Frelt.

These frightening beings, said to range in height from one foot to at least ten, have been spotted lurking in people's gardens and causing panic and disruption to the annual Codge Garden Show and Open Day.

"Where do they come from?" parish council clerk Tweedy Boston asked on Friday and demanded immediate action from district health and safety staff. "It's not good enough," she added. "They have played havoc with our shallots!"

UFO expert Dan Dandridge has speculated that the "visitors" may have been blown off course by a recent meteor shower which passed close to Earth on Sunday and may not have intended to visit our planet. He added: "Be aware, they may be more frightened of us than we are of them. Don't prod them with gardening implements; they may get rather angry..."

Incident referred to at the start of Part One, reprinted by the magazine from the Nobble and Nudge Weekly Times and Advertiser

"Do you believe in flying saucers, they ask? Do you believe in great mysteries? Ghosts? The echoes of trilobites? No! I tell them. I don't believe in flying saucers. They are ridiculous! Listen instead to logic and science. Ghosts? Piffle. Trilobite echoes? What guff! As far as great mysteries, though, I am partial to a nice, knotty Conan Doyle or Agatha Christie..."
Author Chepstow Hawse, interviewed for Twee TV's popular magazine programme *Downalong in the Woods with Your Woofer*.
(Note: This title was misconstrued for some time, but intends to convey *down in the woods with your **dog*** – and not, as some have surmised, accompanied by a collection of speaker cabinet components).

From the Magazine

"The day my basket weaving brought the CIA to my door!" says frightened housewife

the UFO Armageddon

ISSUE #8   £1.00

The
Devastation
Chronicles

Arthur J. Stranzi

The Greatest Dystopian Sci-Fi Novel
of All Time!
A Special Chappie Bonscatho
Report

Here are several pages taken from the few remaining copies of The UFO Armageddon magazine, including (in part three) the issue with the controversial "Stranzi papers."

The cover of this infamous edition has been specially reconstructed by Ephram Twilge, one of the few remaining newsagents (there were only two) to stock the magazine from its launch to its demise.

Twilge told the author: "I remember it well, even though I can't exactly say what it looked like. I know it had the title and a story caption, some aliens and a repro of the novels' book jacket. It was issue eight, certainly*. I know that because my pet hamster was four on the day it came in and I've got two of them."

The author managed to track down the wording of the cover from a footnote in Bonscatho's will in which he left £25 and his collection of pewter penguins to the housewife featured in the issue's upper caption, a lady with whom Bonscatho spent several afternoons discussing the relative values of rattan and hickory and the special popularity of "coiled and plaited" over "twine and splint" whilst enjoying tea, macaroons and the occasional balloon flight.

[*An assertion now known to be false.]

KEEP YOUR
EYES
ON
SKIES
WARNS
TERRIFIED
BISHOP

the UFO Armageddon

ISSUE #7
MAY 89
£1

ABDUCTIONS ISSUE!

They took my husband and left me with a DUCK!

Two-thirds of Wiltshire Council "taken by bright lights..."

This month's tip: Keeping your fish pond Underwater-UFO-free

The story of the Wiltshire parish councillors who allegedly went missing overnight after being attracted by "bright lights" was one of several UFOA stories that were challenged after publication. This case was given "hoax" status after it was claimed that the members involved had not come into contact with a full-on alien encounter, but had only experienced "the bright lights of London" during a coach trip to see The Lion King *in the West End. The Slumps, however, maintained that the story was true and that it did have a UFO connection, based on the "testimony" of a former clerk to the council who was subsequently dismissed from his role for apparently nibbling on a turnip during a parish planning meeting. Adelbald Slump was convinced that the clerk had been "silenced" by "pressure from Ministry officials" and that the incident "stood up" because the village in question was at the heart of the notorious and mysterious "Wiltshire Parallelogram."*

Empty!

Here's an authenticated and candid shot of "The Empty Ones," apparently two delegates of an alien race said to have visited US President Jimmy Carter in 1978 in the Oval Office, shortly after Carter became Commander in Chief of the most powerful handgun nation in the world.

Alien presidential visitors, "Ghostly" actors, or...?

It is not known where the visitors were from, although one Republican wag suggested "Texas." But the gist of the thirty-minute conversation was said to have been about interplanetary trade agreements, possibly about arms, more likely about groceries.

The White House, of course, has always denied that such a meeting took place. One presidential aide, Barrington Dentures, responded to a question from the *New York Times Ten* making reference to alleged trade agreements with the curt: "We ain't selling no grain to no spacemen, nor no guns. American guns stay in America, and so does American corn!"

And it seems he was right.

The reason for the alleged visit is clear. In 1973 Carter formally reported a UFO sighting he had in the late sixties involving a bright white object that changed colour several times (much like a mime stuck in a revolving door), though he added that he did not think it was an alien spacecraft. Even so, Clegg Bimble, one of the dozen or so witnesses, dismissed the customary suggestion that any night-time object seen in the sky is the planet Venus by stating: "Venus does not leap about like a jumping jack, not even when I'm on a rollercoaster!"

Meanwhile, sceptics have dismissed the Empty Ones image herewith as that of two travelling actors taking part in a deliberate "ghostly" hoax to promote their off-Broadway play *Oooh, Spooky!* – and nothing to do with UFOs.

Lead UFO disbeliever and pain in the neck, IT consultant Thred Behr (who lives at home with his mother in Ealing and plays *Space Invaders* in his spare time until his eyes invert), has always claimed that belief in UFOs, in the sense of alien craft, is "unscientific and stupid" and the imaginings of "weak-minded cretins."

Behr, 43, still has his own teddy, drinks only milk and crumbled rusks at his work station, and owns a replica Sinclair C5.

Not so saucy saucer for tunesmiths!

The Arthur Dabbs Skiffle and Croon Concert Party didn't expect their summer performances from the back of a flatbed lorry for an audience of pensioners to attract a larger – alien – audience when they played a selection of tunes from Julian Slade and Dorothy Reynolds' musical *Salad Days* for the Briggington Seniors Sunday Euchre Alliance one August day in 1990.

They were aghast when they saw this picture taken by the circulation manager of their local newspaper the *Brig and Hooser Weekly Rumble* and several members went into hiding until as late as 1996, fearful that the sky was about to fall on them.

Acclaimed spoons virtuoso Mandy Capercaillie remembers the day well.

"I was in a hammock at the back, as my solo was not due for several minutes," she said. "And I glanced over my shoulder at the Barker's chimney which, for once, wasn't belching out black smoke as the Barkers like to roast mink on their Aga and often forget about them until the fur starts smeeching.

"Anyway, I was the first to see the object which looked like two of Aunt Minnie's soup dishes, but metallic and glued together, edge to edge. I don't know if it made a sound because the band was just concluding – ironically, wouldn't you say – *The Saucer Song*!

"Well, I can tell you this saucer was anything but saucy! And by the time they'd finished it had gone and no-one believed me until Jack Prodderboast from the *Rumble* produced his print of the moment and, my, they were all a-flummoxed!"

Footnote.
The song referred to here recalls a "flying dish." Nobody, they sing,
ever saw "such a saucy saucer." This recalls a phrase often used by the
Bernard Pledge Centre for UFO Studies and Fruit Farm
currently based in a small shack on Selsey Bill, West Sussex.

Thirties picnic party materialises at modern-day Stonehenge!

— Locals shocked

HUNDREDS of sightseers were shocked to see a picnic party from the 1930s suddenly materialise at Britain's most famous monument on Tuesday. An equally stunned pre-war Gladys Pembroke said: "I think it must have been the jasmine tea," though experts are talking about "wormholes." The party of four vanished after thirty minutes and a bag of crisps each.
(See page 5)

This story was a favourite of Maurice Slump, who claimed to have been present when the incident occurred and able to verify its veracity, despite claims from rival UFO publication Whoosh! *that it was a fabrication.*

TUFOA ran a weekly column of stories that set out to debunk every extraterrestrial encounter ever reported. Here is one of them.

This week: The "Real" Area 51!

Extensive investigations by Californian UFO expert Chester Cheesemaker have claimed to show the "REAL TRUTH" behind the rumours about the mythological Area 51 military compound in the Nevada desert where contemporary legend says alien craft and bodies are stored. In 1992 Cheesemaker released details of his findings on the so-called "secret base."

He told his local newspaper: "Well, I took the truck and I went up to the NO ENTRY signs, up there around where it is, round 130 kilometers north-Northwest of LA. I saw the usual white SUV on a hillside, like they was a'watchin me, but I took no notice.

"All those warnings about PROCEED AND YOU DIE just didn't add up. I know they was hiding something, so I drove off bout half a mile an parked up, then waited til dark an made my own way over the hills and ridges, deeper into the desert til I found what they didn't want us to see. It was daybreak by then, and I took the photo."

He added: "All those years of denial and deceit to find that there's NOTHIN out there: no clandestine air force base testing top secret aircraft, no flyin saucers, no spacemen. Only a dilapidated stone hut with two old prospectors (who were hiding inside and wouldn't show themselves due to their long beards) and a pair of lawn chairs. Boy, was that an eye-opener!"

Cheesemaker also dismissed the alleged clandestine activities of the associated Edwards Air Force Base, adding: "Or, as we old hands call it, *Teds*. Just a collection of harmless old planes on harmless old World War Two style runways. It's more of a museum than a site for intrigue and conspiracy."

He added: "It's a real friendly place, and the public are always welcome to pop in for a coffee, a chat and an Eccles cake, specially imported from the good ole U of K."

Teds Air Force Base, apparently pictured in 2008,
where public are encouraged to "pop in"

In a TUFOA footnote, from an article headed *The Folly of Lies*, Bonscatho writes: "Chester Cheesemaker, 88, is a former NSA disinformation specialist and one-time personal advisor to Senator Joe *'string them Commies up'* McCarthy and therefore his testimony is at best doubtful and at worst downright doo doo."

Bonscatho added, rather superfluously, that he had a pair of lawn chairs just like those in the picture which he bought from his local garden centre and, ominously – though obtusely – they were *"made in China!!!"*

Children's Corner: A Gripping Yarn

One of the first children's stories to touch on the UFO question was Emily Parsnip's 1952 outing *Binky's Dilemma*, from the popular magazine *Girls' Jolly Weekend Revels*.

A group of spunky school chums discover a piece of an alien spacecraft in the grounds of their rural boarding school. Head girl Binky Clandestine agonises over whether she should tell the Ministry of Defence, or even their kindly biology mistress. Could their dangerous find land them in hot water? Is there a crashed saucer, or even a space man, hiding in the school grounds? Will they solve the mysteries before their periods begin? Crikey!

Final Edition Jan 99

the UFO ARMAGEDDON

Special Farewell Edition £1.75

Space Wars: It's Real and Happening Now!

Cheltenham could be in flames by Christmas says fireman

*For its final edition, UFOA went for an all-out shocker.
In its stories based largely on the 1956 film* Earth vs the Flying Saucers, *the Slumps set out to prove that not only had some of the population been taken over by carnivorous newts, but a vast alien invasion fleet was hiding behind Saturn with a forward base on the dark side of the moon. The theory proved to be unfounded following judicious use of the Mauna Kea Observatory in Hawaii and several sets of Swarovski binoculars. Even so, in 2002 Alelbald was still inaugurated into the Daffid Yike School of Fly Munchers as its resident UberKook for his UFO services.*

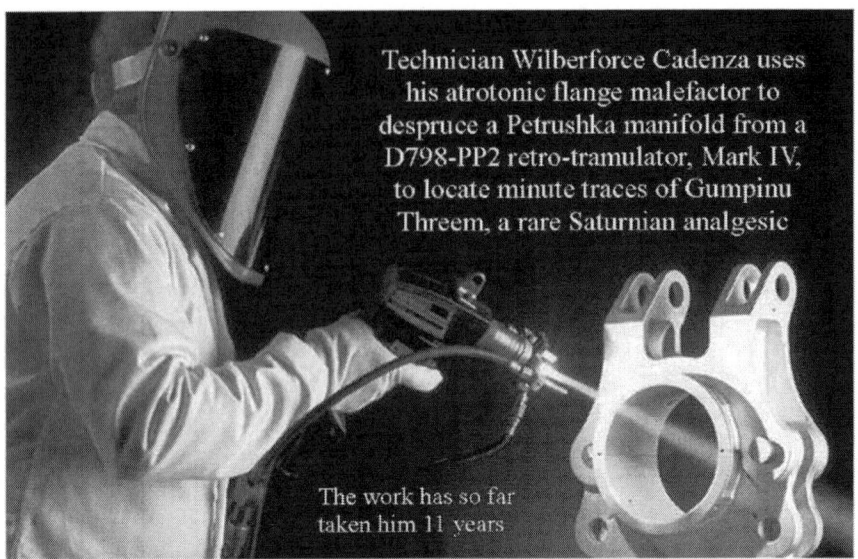

Technician Wilberforce Cadenza uses his atrotonic flange malefactor to despruce a Petrushka manifold from a D798-PP2 retro-tramulator, Mark IV, to locate minute traces of Gumpinu Threem, a rare Saturnian analgesic

The work has so far taken him 11 years

Flying saucer hunters Ray Spring and Augustine Moo utilise the latest sonic ET-detector gun to spot those ever-elusive UFOs

Ray is an experienced hen juggler and Augustine raises sheep (by levitation)

Their special equipment, paid for by their local UFO Group, is able to detect any unusual movements in cloud formations, rock strata and tapioca pudding

The illustrated headings to two UFOA features, now lost

Film Review!

Mess (Certificate X)
Starring Clegg Mowcher and Bruna Pipp, directed by Jerry Hassenbach,
colour, 92 minutes

Johnny Mucklesnatch, a Harvard graduate, has spent the last three years investigating the life, lore and leaves of plants. He is convinced that human tissue and plant tissue are compatible. This proves to be his first biological error, the major mistake in his life, and the tenuous basis for this film's plot (a well-chosen word, under the agronomical circumstances). One night at the College of Floral Speculation he injects himself with the essence of sunflower. There are no visible effects for the next few days, with the exception that he grows several inches which he hides by lowering the heels on his loafers. His girl friend Eva, however, spots the difference. "Gee, Johnny," she says. "You've grown several inches." "Have I?" he replies, evasively.

One evening Johnny's aged tutor Phineas Phrogg calls him and suggests they meet at his apartment to discuss their separate theories about plant evolution. It sounds like as truly fascinating evening. Johnny goes along, bringing dips. But as he gets to Phrogg's apartment he is overcome by dizziness and wakes up the next morning in his own flat covered in leaves. Surprised by this agricultural occurrence, Johnny picks up the *Los Angeles Herald* and finds a story on page one that freezes his stamen. Dr Phrogg has been killed in the night. Neighbours talk of a giant sunflower leaving the premises. The police from twenty seven neighbouring districts have been alerted.

After three more surprise killings the police become more intensive in their search for *"The Mess,"* Eva wonders where her lover has disappeared to, and Johnny sprouts facial petals and grows to 11ft 6ins. It becomes unbearable living in his flat, so he goes to the college and plants himself in their vivarium.

There he becomes friendly with a Nevada cactus and the pair dream of plants taking over the world. They leave the vivarium, with a few friendly mangoes, and seek solace and plans in the nearby wasteland. They gather a huge army of plants and march on Los Angeles. But, in order that the film doesn't breach the copyright of *The Tray of the Diffids*, they are thwarted as they approach Hollywood when a huge duck, bred by the Department of Aquatic Warfare, San Francisco, swoops down and devours the entire army.

The city is now faced with a new problem: decorate the duck for its valiant action in saving the community or destroy it before it goes too far. They decided to destroy it. But as their squadron of nuclear bombers approach the duck, peacefully grazing in 75 acres of pasture land, the sky is split apart by the deafening shriek of a seventy ton wren, which pounces on the duck, squashing it to death. Suddenly, before the bombers can change course to intercept the new menace, a fifty mile long water snake bursts out of the North Pacific Ocean, devours the wren, smashes down the aircraft, and elects itself Governor of California.

But, before it can take office, the ground opens up in the biggest earthquake since the eponymous film and the snake falls into a huge pit. The pit actually goes right to the centre of the Earth which has been populated for centuries by a vast tribe of mutant locksmiths who kill, burn and pillage their way across the planet until they all catch flu and die.

And that's just the first twenty-two minutes...

Also on limited release is the exotic Bulgarian animated cartoon *Halva*, directed by Stotz Quoit, creator of *The Boy Who Dropped a Mine Down His Trousers and Now Walks With a Limpet.*

This 56-minute feature (*illustrated below with some individual frames*) is created entirely in black and white by a team of 137 animators using special cake-proof mapping pens and inks made traditionally from lampblack, soot and pig fat. It took them 17 years to complete.

Reviews!
They're Coming...!

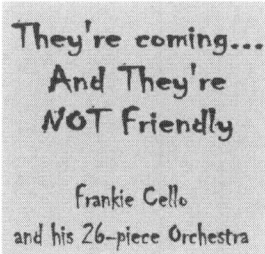

They're Coming and They're Not Friendly! is the latest CD from the busy composer-musician Frankie Cello. This new release on the Whimsical label features *Frankie Cello and his 26-piece Orchestra* – which turns out to be just Cello himself (not his real name) and a euphonium.

The album, a full 59 minutes of anguished songs and spirited puffing, is the third part of Cello's "Cosmos trilogy," which began with the optimistic *Cello: How Are You?* with a cover shot of the artist shaking "hands" with an astral traveller, and continued with *Life is Just a Bolas Cello*, a less confident outing with a cover picture of Cello falling towards the camera looking surprised, his ankles entangled by the strings of the popular Argentinian weighted throwing device with the thrower's webbed and non-human hand clearly in shot.

This time, though, the gloves are really off: aliens are bad, there's no making friends with them, and the planet – that's OUR planet – could be doomed to subservience in the next millennium or even The Next Twenty Two Minutes (the title of one of the songs which predicts the swift downfall of human civilisation by a warrior extraterrestrial race and was written after a weekend Cello spent viewing all the *Alien* films). The cover is blood red, one plain colour, with the title and artist in a deeper shade of red, representing the carnage Cello sees on the horizon.

In order to circumvent various potential issues under the Trades Description Act, Cello says that his claim of a "26-piece orchestra" performing his tunes is valid as his specially-adapted single instrument consists of twenty six separate brass pieces. These pieces are disassembled by him at the end of each performance and reassembled before the commencement of the next, thereby allowing him to generate a slightly different tone for each recital and also to clean out all the congealed spit from the previous outing.

An early Barlington Snig pencil portrait of Cello when he was first tuba in the Compunctious Wind Ensemble. Sketch after Gerard Hoffnung but before lunch.

Asked why he chose the euphonium as his instrument of choice –
especially with the almost insurmountable difficulties of accompanying
himself on a wind instrument whilst singing – Cello replies: "The cold
brass and the languid and haunting baritone timbre of the euphonium
creates an almost piquant atmosphere within a cerulean ambience; a milieu
of oceanic swells creating a prevailing mood of perhaps indigo
prescience."

And we've all been there at some time, haven't we?

Children's Corner: Spaceman Poetry
Extract from opening poem *The Visitor in* Kernet Vanilakone's
new collection of kids' verse, *Off We Go Again*

The spaceship landed in the Square
With a hiss and a flash of fire
The Mayor came out of his council flat
With his nightgown pinned with wire.
He crossed to the shimmering silver ball
With his eyeballs wet with dew
Then a scaly man with a horny tail
Stepped slowly into view.
He scanned a swiftly-growing crowd
With a look half glazed with pity
Then the Mayor approached the stranger
And gave him the key to the city.

The Mystery of the Venusian Fly

Eight-year-old Tarquin Ninny caused a stir in his Cumberland town when he told his parents that a "funny fairy" had taken the tooth he had secreted under his pillow and left him "a new, shiny sixpence." When he was asked how funny this tooth fairy had been – did he wear a red nose, fold balloons or tell Xmas cracker jokes? – Tarquin drew this sketch which he named the "Venusian Fly." Both his immediate neighbours and nearby UFO group (Jerry Bunt-Milverne's Skywatchers) were equally shocked and intrigued by the incident and a serious investigation was launched into just what Tarquin had seen in the dead of night in his room.

This continued for eight months until father Gabardine Ninny admitted that (a) he had accidentally knocked his son's tooth out during a tussle over some frozen peas, and (b) that to make up for the "regrettable" scuffle he had delivered the coin himself at 2am dressed in a ridiculous "monster" outfit from his ailing costume hire firm. Hearing the news, Tarquin complained: "You could have given me more than sixpence!"

Was Mr Ninny genuine in his explanation?

Or had he been "got at" by officers of the Scafell Pike trading standards department, a known front for anti-UFO black ops in the North of England, according to the Unidentified Surveillance Executive Liaison East-South Sector chief Lt-Col Bashford Strontium (TA)?

Editor's footnote. Following this incident Gabardine Ninny fled the country and was last heard of running a Pampas grass cutting service near Cordoba, Argentina dressed as a pantomime llama. Tarquin Ninny changed his name to Gruyere and became a "big cheese" in the stock market, accruing many "shiny sixpences" in a career spanning at least a fortnight. The Scafell Pike trading standards department was mysteriously closed following publication of the above article and allegedly relocated to "somewhere in the Solway Firth."

**I'm a Space fella
space-filler**

Sigh...

"Bod"

After the collapse of their friendship and their magazine, Maurice and Adelbald Slump went their own ways. Maurice disappeared after joining a commune and was rumoured to have spent his latter days tending goats in a mountainous region of Andalusia.

Adelbald briefly became a cartoonist, publishing his work (of which there was very little) under the pseudonym "Bod." He began a light-hearted alien visitation strip tentatively called Ag and Dag, pitching it for *The Guardian* newspaper.

The strip ran for just one episode (*previous page*), and even that was "pulled" from the second edition due to its incomprehensible captions.

Slump admitted that he could not understand his own captions, which did not help his creative case, going on to claim that the language came to him in a "vision" during a Bridlington donkey ride.

"Bod" began his own comic book, *SNURK*, planned as a multi-volume sci-fi epic, but was only able to complete one page before being evicted by his landlord for stealing a tea cake. He was to spend the rest of his artistic career painting yellow No Parking lines.

Opposite is the only page of Bod's proposed epic comic book SNURK, which was accepted for publication during a lunch at Burgers-4-All by the head of *Absolutely! Comics* but rejected when Slump took eighteen months to come up with this first panel.

"Bod was planning a six-book epic of around forty pages per issue," said AC MD J. C. Dee. "But, at this rate, it would've taken best part of a century to get to the end, and I reckoned that might just have been around 95 years too long."

Instead Dee optioned Joe Dongo's *Parsnip Man*, which was already complete. But sadly issue one failed to sell a single copy and Dee gave up the comic book trade and went back to his first love, plastering.

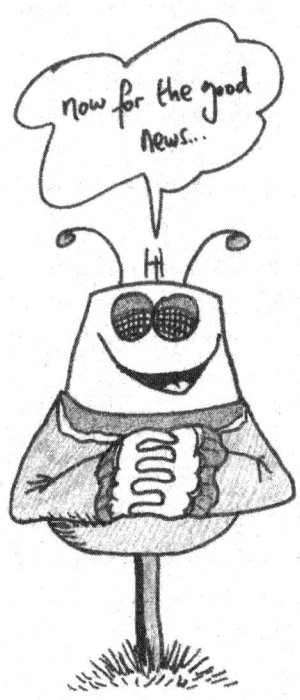

Popular character heading UFOA's Happy Encounters *column where readers tell their tales of positive meetings with aliens, such as the Cottoncoddie crofter who claims a "grey" helped him pull his beets and his wife prod her clootie mats.*

PART THREE

The Stranzi Papers

"Tuesday means more to me than a buckwheat hat, a sourdough chalice and the buttery aroma of a perfect brioche with chardonnay. Yet, Tuesday was when I had my first alien encounter. They were small, green, and scaly and, though common sense and wit tells me they were merely natural lizards I felt that the neatly-laced spats and bobble hats were significant."

Actor Cabley Snoop, article from *Whoops, They're Bonkers (Or Are They?)*, the magazine for the over-privileged.

One Last Word: The Stranzi Papers!

There follows the complete Chappie Bonscatho essay for *TUFOA* on the long-lost novels of Arthur J. Stranzi. It marks the only time that virtually an entire edition of the magazine was devoted to one subject, which occurred whilst the Slumps were in Tuscany on a painting course leaving their co-writer in charge as editor.

Bonscatho had previously become a fanatical devotee of the reclusive Stranzi and the author's sole mega-work and had scoured the world for copies of the separate books and the breeze-block-sized single volume (which he found in Turkey just after a careless antiquarian bookseller had attempted to use it as stuffing for an antique sofa).

Stranzi's epic became one of the epics of the magazine itself and attracted a huge postbag of nearly five letters (the fifth was accidentally eaten, unread, by Bonscatho's borzoi when it dropped from the letterbox into his pet's feeding bowl). The Slumps found the undue and, in their estimation, unwarranted attention bestowed on Bonscatho was a tad irksome and within a week of their return, tanned and weighed down with canvasses of orange-tinged country villas and stalky cypress trees, they had taken back the reins of *TUFOA* and Bonscantho was retired to the countryside. The Stranzi issue was pulped and this author has only been able to track down one copy, sans its cover.

Still, Bonscatho's Stranzi review attracted reviews of its own, and here is just a handful. Well, three.

The Stranzi Review Reviews!

"Extraordinary. Bonscatho manages to match Stranzi's fiction perfectly, creating a review that surpasses even the tediousness of the prose he so admires..."
Lenton Flange, *Books and More Books: Tomes for the Times*

"I was drawn to the tragic life and work of Stranzi like a moth to an oxy acetylene welding torch and was subsequently quite blinded by Bonscatho's innate ability to shine the attention on the printed page, as if engaging the fuel gases and oxygen of creativity in a wholly new way. Three thousand five hundred degrees of pure HEAT from this most heliocentric of reviewers, at the true core of his subject and the sharp and polished apex of his craft..."
Desmonde Paunch, "Spurious Weekends," *Pretentious Times and Gazette*

"The review of the life of Stranzi (Jugling) is a review in itself, whereas the plotting of the three books latterly reviewed reflects a more desolate version of Orwell's *1984*, a despairing reflection of Tolkein's *Lord of the Rings* and a nondescript recapturing of Moorcock's Burroughs-influenced *Eternal Champion* worlds. How I miss *Bunty* and Enid Blighton..."
Germaine Elizabeth Clove-Tappet, *Libraries, Book Clubs and Tea Cosies Weekly*

The Zerstörung Saga:

A re-evalution by Chappie Bonscatho

Arthur J. Stranzi

DESOLATION

The Author (real name Terrence Jugling, left) and the first of his unique, bleak trio of linked sci-fi novels that sold badly when he self-published in the 1950s but went on to net him the prestigious, Pumice Slab Award (for unique, bleak, sci-fi trilogies) when re-published posthumously as *The Devastation Chronicles* by Cornashop Paperbacks in 1989.

I first came across the dystopian world of Arthur J. Stranzi while I was a mature student at Frankenheimer Technical College in Hull. I recall that my flatmate, a former plumber who was taking a short course in particle physics, was rolling a joint on a battered paperback and discussing Kierkegaard with a Bosnian apple-picker (reading contemporary fisheries), when the revelation came.

I was unaccountably drawn to this odd little book with no front cover, which I swiftly pilfered from my co-tenant once he was glassy-eyed and staring intently at a small, sample square of maroon flock wallpaper he had stapled to his headboard. The strangely-compelling plot précis on the back of the limp little tome, speckled with tobacco strands, screamed of alien invasion, death and inescapable horror, reminding me so much of my early days in Ipswich as a trainee welder – its succinct, almost epigrammatic white-on-grey descriptive text illustrated with a scratchy monochrome image of smoking rubble sucking away at a charred and up-turned ceramic sink, seemingly dragging that symbol of domestic reliability, of comfortable, identifiable and invariable reassurance, down into the veritable pits of Dante's Hell. I was shocked, I was humbled, and I was hooked.

I checked out the name on the title page: Arthur J. Stranzi. I'd never heard of him. But there was something about the name, the way it rolled off the tongue with an unfamiliar burr, yet still a rich vein of assurance, accompanied in the same intake of breath with a sense that its owner was bequeathing the reader with a brooding ethereal blanket of menace to accompany him through his reading experience, should he choose to follow the fallow brick road.

The book was a yellowing copy of Stranzi's opening salvo of his gripping, epic trilogy, succinctly and, it turned out, appropriately entitled *Desolation*. For its cruel, remorseless path reflected the isolation (oddly enough, the title of its first sequel) and bitter friendlessness that I had felt since moving from my home town to a new, yet thankfully temporary perch in my corner of a seemingly cheerless, colourless metropolis which always seemed to smell of fish.

I consumed *Desolation's* awful story in one sitting, without food, liquid, sleep or associated body functions: I truly became one of its tangled plot's victims, running from the fear and the killing, the monsters, the increasingly unhinged and panic-stricken populous and the constant threat of rabid dogs, cats, and screaming, swooping pigeons (once partly domesticated, now brutally feral).

It was an experience I would never forget and I eagerly began seeking out Stranzi's other volumes – he only ever wrote three books – along with anything biographical I could find out about the man. Sadly, or perhaps inevitably, this was at the expense of my studies, which fell so much by the wayside that, by the third term I had been stripped of my scholarship and chased off campus by the college security team of two testosterone-charged gardeners and a one-legged electrician. I didn't care. I had found both my new Utopia, and its nemesis, in one (un)healthy bite. My future was set.

I discovered that Stranzi, born in 1910 to a Dorchester bridle-maker and his fulsome wife, a Yeovil farmer's daughter and renowned goat milker, did not start writing until he was 42 when he was successfully, though rather mundanely, established as a booking clerk at a small halt on a branch line of the Somerset and Dorset Railway. It seems to have been stirred by the monotony of daily life at the two-man stop comprising one bellicose Puddletown-born signalman who refused to talk to his colleague, or to even leave his box, and Stranzi himself, engaged as clerk and general man of all trades.

Of course, he was not called Stranzi then, and, in fact, never was called Stranzi beyond the universe of his three books. Further, no-one ever knew that the mild-mannered booking clerk with the *en brosse* moustache and

soprano voice (acquired through a throat injury from a shoddily-lobbed shuttlecock) was even a writer. For Stranzi was born Terrence Muddlehouse Jugling, and remained Terrence Jugling for the extent of his days, refusing to acknowledge the Muddlehouse part of his name, appended to his life's appellation by parents anxious to appease a despised uncle who they hoped would leave them his butchery business in grateful response. (They were sorely disappointed in this goal.)

Jugling (who I will hereafter mostly refer to by his artistic alias alone) escaped military service during World War Two, firstly by hiding, and then by claiming conscientious objection, next by medical pronouncement (his feet were less flat as duck-like) and finally through working in a reserved occupation, serving some six years in a lighthouse. He moved on to the railways in 1946, met his future wife in 1947, who left him for a door-to-door Kleeneze salesman two months after the ceremony and was last heard of running a guest house for travelling thespians in Bognor Regis.

The unexpected author wrote his extraordinary and vibrant trilogy – as previously outlined, his only published work – between ticket sales, hunched at a desk in his wooden stationmaster's shack, setting down the bulk of its 3,241 pages in pencil in a series of leather travel journals over two successive winters in 1952 and 1953. No-one knows why he began the daunting task (merely positing boredom in his work), nor why he chose the prophetic genre of science fiction. The first of the three volumes, *Desolation*, was published the following spring and the remaining two parts, the stark *Isolation* and the terrifying *Annihilation*, in January and October 1955 respectively. All three books reflect the harsh conditions and the loneliness of an interminable succession of bleak nights spent in a draughty hut on a desolate West Country railway platform with only a two-bar electric fire, a small blanket, some cheese sandwiches and a stuffed parrot for company.

He took the initial manuscript to a modest publishing house in nearby Salisbury, specialising in coin collecting, but found it almost immediately rejected by its owner, one Arthur Quilt, a surly gentleman who Jugling first encountered during the exchange of a threepenny ticket to Blandford for a bag of Kettlering's mothballs (*no explanation is given for this curious transaction in my source researches*). Quilt declined the novel on the grounds that it was "grossly violent and unremittingly depressing and not the kind of thing people want to read whilst cradled in a seaside deck chair in August."

But Stranzi pressed on regardless and, due to a small benefaction received following the unexpected demise of Uncle Muddlehouse (a rather unsavoury end apparently caused by one of his own meat slicers), he was able to self-publish *Desolation* – and, subsequently its two sequels – appropriating the unaccommodating Quilt's forename as part of his spicy new pseudonym.

UK sales were small, bookshops showed little interest and the author was often forced to display his cherished handiwork on trestle tables at village fetes or in local market halls next to fruit and vegetable stalls, and the final instalment was nearly abandoned when Stranzi went through a period of insecurity and self-loathing only rivalled by Jean Paul Sartre's extended doleful gaze into the abyss between pages 123 and 141 of his masterwork *La Nausee* when protagonist Roquentin, realising that inanimate objects are indifferent to human existence, spends four days discussing both phenomenologist epistemology and carrot cake recipes with his toaster in an attempt to obtain a response – a section later excised from the manuscript. The French existentialist (pictured) subsequently warned: "If you are lonely when you are alone, you are in bad company. But if you are alone when you are alone, then you are truly alone, comprehensively lonely and yet, as alone, therefore in no company at all, except for my friend Françoise who has a hat shop."

Remarkably, Stranzi's books only took off when they were published in Germany through the auspices of a philanthropic Austrian timber merchant who had been staying with relatives in Portland when he came across *Desolation* (the book) in a doctor's waiting room. He tracked down the author, obtained the rights to republish, handed the manuscript to a translator and the resultant re-named *Zerstörung Chronicles* became a small-scale sensation in both Dortmund and Essen, two communities still recovering from wartime bombing that found an empathetic ambience in Stranzi's intense, frenetic prose of loss, destruction, hopelessness and charred railway timetables.

F I N A L L Y, in 1989, the eclectic Cornashop Paperbacks – known mostly for esoteric titles such as *Yoga For Roofers, Introducing Schoenberg to Under-Fives* and the comic *Even Mice Dig Shinto!* – bit the publishing bullet and re-issued the entire Stranzi trilogy in one volume, re-translated back from the German edition.

The Devastation Chronicles was picked up by the prestigious periodical *Bookie Book Bods,* where a 32-line review by writer's doyen and essayist Numsen Popleaf led to interest from *The Science Fiction, Fantasy and Horror Writer's and Reader's Sporadic Journal* (the SFFHWRSJ) and it was just a matter of weeks before the breeze-block-sized tome came under the eagle eye of P.P. Floater, a popular critic of comics, graphic novels, sci-fi, fantasy and fruit bottling magazines, who was also the instigator of the prestigious Pumice Slab Award. In a stroke, he redirected the 2000 gong to the work of Arthur J. Stranzi, coincidentally marking what would have been the author's 90th birthday. Sadly, the epic adventure continued to sell badly, a projected film deal with Momentary Films fell apart and within a matter of months *Desolation, Isolation* and *Annihilation* were out of print once more.

THE brief sortie with Cornashop came about through a curious intervention by one Adam Endseat, son of Jugling's first, only and short-lived wife, who came across the German bumper edition of the saga in a backstreet second hand bookshop in Hamburg in 1996 whilst on a mature student's gap year to study both the language and the making of labskaus, an interesting culinary dish mixing corned beef with herring, beetroot, mashed potato, pickled cucumber and fried eggs in the hope that it might catch on as a breakfast treat in his elderly mother's Bognor B&B.

Endseat (*pictured as a lad*) was shocked to learn from a local bibliophile and mat-weaver that the author was in fact English and, more to the point, the man who could have been his father had the mild-mannered Terrence Jugling ever got round to fathering him, rather than leaving that task to a transitory ventriloquist whose four-week engagement at an end-of-the-pier summer show in Bognor was cut short by tonsillitis and a recuperative bunk-up with Adam Endseat's mother at the family lodgings.

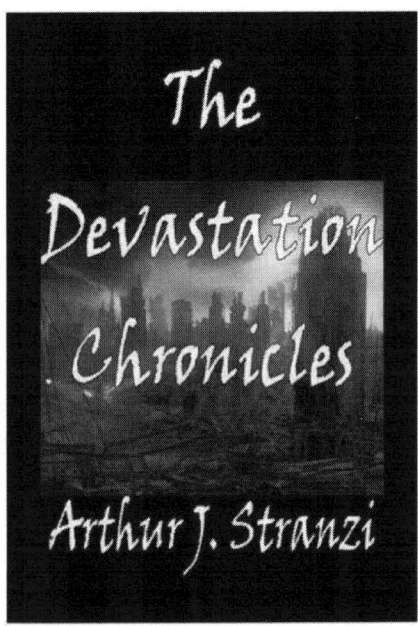

The Devastation Chronicles

Arthur J. Stranzi

NEXT ISSUE

Chelmsford man finds alien creature in his attic

"I don't know how it got there," plasterer Cardew Goskoheeli

tells *UFOA*. "But there was a meteor shower last night and it could've come down the chimney. Listen to it squeak. It doesn't bite!"

The Review!

(Warning to readers: Contains important plot disclosures)

The first book, *Desolation*, tells of a vicious attack on Earth by a fleet of alien craft. The planet's population is decimated by the ruthlessness of these strange new flying machines, though it turns out the attack is not by visitors from another world, but by Earth's own, newly-established World Government whose leaders plan to eliminate poverty by eliminating the poor, leaving the land for the elite. They use a highly-sophisticated new technology, including "invisible" attack planes, designed and built by former Nazi engineers in secret underground labs in Nevada, USA, the Urals and the Cairngorms National Park.

The story is told through the eyes of bricklayer Jack Hanniband, a former train driver, whose main line station was one of the first buildings to be demolished in a concerted attack on his Romford home. His wife was unaccountably smothered by chewing gum just hours before the "alien" war so, completely alone, Jack becomes an outlaw, gathering together other survivors and escaping the city through sewers, sinkholes and drainage ditches. At the dead of night they hole up in a wooded refuge, armed with gear looted from abandoned tackle shops and armouries.

From the book!

A runner was seen, diving between the trenches and the craters of the ravaged lowlands towards the hidden refuge on a hill, screened for the moment behind a band of surviving trees harshly silhouetted against a watery, smog-smeared sun. A spotter with binoculars crouching in a copse of singed hawthorn confirmed it was Chay Sweedy, known to the survivors as "Marksman."

Sweedy arrived at the secret lair, sweaty and panting; his face streaked with blood, mud and slime, his home-made crossbow and quiver of stunted arrows swinging loosely at his side, and made straight for Jack Hanniband, commander of the Southern Renegades. He adjusted his tattered camouflage jacket and gave his leader a tired salute.

"They've wiped out Droitwich," he gasped, his throat betraying the cracked rasp of exhaustion, lack of water and food and the creeping onset of leukaemia.

"Droitwich?" Hanniband responded. He slapped the broken rifle butt clutched firmly in his right hand against his artificial left leg, the result of a dreadful skirmish six months earlier that had led to the fatal maiming of three hundred of his best men.

"Men, women, children. Every last one," Sweedy said, shaking his head in regret. "Everyone, everything, down to the last kitten."

"Bastards!" Hanniband growled.

"Even the bastards," Sweedy sighed, thinking of Hanniband's own son Clint, cruelly born out of wedlock and now lost somewhere in Chingford – wounded, perhaps already dead, certainly out of the fight.

For now, at least. He knew Hanniband had a plan for the safe return of Clint and the vital map that his son had stolen which gave a detailed floor plan of the headquarters of the Enemy: a document that would guide a final ground assault for the Southern Renegades – a death-or-glory last stand.

In **book two**, *Isolation*, the survivors band together to destroy the UK sector of the new World Government, having discovered the awful truth at the end of book one. Through a Citizen's Band radio network they have linked with other pockets of resistance in other parts of the world, where similar attacks are taking place.

From the book!

Jack Hanniband, now short of an arm he lost at the Norwich Rout and an eye taken at the Morecambe Sands Debacle, stared at himself in the gold framed mirror on a reception room wall at the British President's palatial suite in underground Central London.

Hanniband was tired, exhausted, close to defeated, but not yet ready to throw in the towel; he looked his age, war etched into every crack and crevice of his parchment-yellow skin. In that moment, that brief hiatus from the dreadful storm of the last two years, he remembered the final days of his short-lived lover Samantha, who had perished in the heart rending chip pan incident; also the plucky stance of his son Clint, blasted apart by an exploding moped as he hurled the vital map showing the layout of the Enemy's covert headquarters toward his father with the cry: "Save us! Save us all."

Grasping the machine pistol tightly in his scarred right hand, ready to use it at any moment, Hanniband turned to the frightened but still defiant man lashed to the leather chair, his grey suit flecked with dust and blood; not his blood, not the blood of the President himself, but the blood of the sixteen aides who fell defending their master.

President George Crossley-Paddington, a self-seeking Tory degenerate who had gained the highest position in the land through a combination of ruthlessness, barbarism, sexual perversion and cannibalism. Not something he'd declared on the Party Manifesto the last time any form of public elections had been held, Hanniband thought grimly.

Book three, *Annihilation*, begins in the wake of the destruction of the World Government by its own disenchanted people – bands of rebels like Jack's post-apocalyptic crew. But there is no time to rejoice or to re-establish a stable democracy as, on the very day the last World Government stronghold collapses in China, the real spaceships arrive.

This race of merciless beings has been closely monitoring the political situation on Earth and they now set about dispatching the exhausted survivors of their planet-wide civil war with clinical expediency. There is virtually no resistance. They achieve supremacy by launching a canopy of explosive devices [*similar to today's thermobaric bombs* – Editor] which kill the remaining humans through a gigantic pressure wave which sucks away from the face of the planet all the oxygen, a gas the aliens do not need to survive.

From the book!

Jack felt his insides quiver, then bulge, and suddenly they were outside. He felt himself looking down at his internal organs strewn across the supermarket car park and wondered how and why as the air sucked out of his lungs and joined them on the tarmac. It was the last thing this one-eyed hero, now legless and confined to a handcart, ever saw of the world, his world that was, as it turned dark for the last time. A dog barked – his faithful Rocky, still at his side – then turned inside out with a fatal hiss.

Around them the buildings, road signs and street furniture remained undamaged in the wake of the devastating, yet selective bomb blast. The empty supermarket, which had been holding an exhibition of experimental art before the Greatest War, looked sad and grey; its huge hoarding advertising the *ADSA DADA Retrospective* now seemed to mock the expired and twisted forms of its one-time customers littering the silent concourse.

Surviving military chiefs, politicians and business executives that have taken refuge in submarines or underground bunkers around the globe are routed when the oceans and land masses are sieved by a massive supplementary energy surge generated by thousands of aerial devices stationed in the (former) atmosphere and controlled by the aliens' grand command vessel orbiting the Moon. With all human and animal life on the planet extinguished, the aliens move in, along with their partners and their pets, and begin rebuilding the planet to their liking.

But their triumph is short-lived. For an unexpected asteroid the size of Mount Everest hits the Earth within days of their arrival and all life is extinguished for good. Earth, now a glowing, barren rock, then destabilises, careers out of orbit into its own Moon and ping-pongs the cracked mass across the galaxy to collide with Mars. This creates a ripple effect throughout the Milky Way causing the impacted galaxy to lose position and crash into an adjoining star cluster, destroying both (including, ironically, the alien invader's original home, now completely vacated).

This catastrophe sets off a chain reaction that causes the very Universe itself to explode and then just as rapidly implode, leaving an empty vacuum. The final sound in the Universe is a small pop as the last of its unique matter disappears, awaiting another Big Bang before beginning the process all over again, in a millennium or two.

The ultimate UFO Armageddon...

Actual Author's Note

My special thanks to the late P. J. Gretton for his important research into the amazing story of Norfolk butcher Harry Widdlescombe, to K. Salter and S. Geatches for their invaluable input into the provocative Pipp/Blake magazine interview, and to M. J. Dunn for the sticky Guinness pudding. It is to these four members of the short-lived but exceptional Onesheep Five comedy group that this little booklet is dedicated.

This playful parody is inspired by all those "serious" TV documentaries about the UFO Phenomenon which remorselessly ridicule the subject with loads of less-than-credible "witnesses;" also all those deluded folk whose stories make for such entertaining listening, including all the debunkers, satirists and blatant fraudsters, those authors who present colourful assumptions as facts; and all the serious researchers who swim upstream constantly in a sea of information, disinformation, misinformation and self-aggrandisement.

I have no idea whether craft and creatures from other planets exist, or if they have ever visited this exceptional globe. But it would seem very sad (and most unlikely) if we were alone in such a gigantic Universe. I can say that I have personally seen several unidentified items in the sky over the years, including one classic "cigar-shaped" object, clearly outlined against the cloudless blue and floating past in an unconcerned way.

There are those who have experienced UFO encounters that they cannot explain – some of them quite sane, their apparent encounters terrifying – in amongst the rank-and-file believers and a legion of happy kooks and deceivers.

For those wanting to take a serious look at the subject, may I recommend the finely-researched works of author/musician Timothy Good.

Acknowledgements

Most images in this book are drawn by the author , taken from the author's personal photo collection, or culled from copyright-free sources. Some sources are unknown. Here are some acknowledgements of other sources.

Alien creature model, Ann Louise; cornfield UFO, fullhdpictures.com; cave paintings, Pete Gretton; Ludicrous Amiander image (Petrarch), pinterest.com; poo fighter, daileyint.com (SBD Douglas dive bomber); original, unadulterated Somerset saucer main photo, Andrew Rees; unadulterated *A Gripping Yarn* illustration, *Our Girls' Tip Top*, artist unknown.

Any copyright holder wishing to be mentioned in any future editions of this book should contact the author.

By the author of

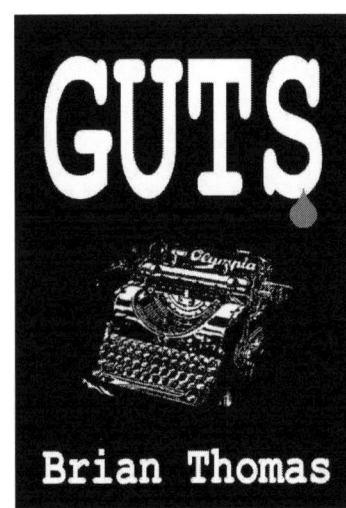

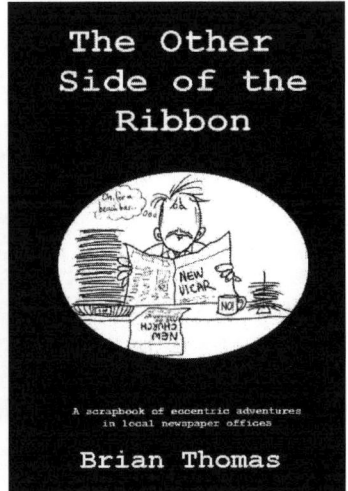

Available from Amazon or CreateSpace

Printed in Great Britain
by Amazon